MEN IN STITCHES

MEN IN STITCHES

Robert E. Illes

VAN NOSTRAND REINHOLD COMPANY
New York Cincinnati Toronto London Melbourne

Dedicated to Those of You Who Intend to Stay Young

Van Nostrand Reinhold Company Regional Offices:
New York Cincinnati Chicago Millbrae Dallas
Van Nostrand Reinhold Company International Offices:
London Toronto Melbourne

Photographs and drawings by the author unless credited otherwise

Published by Van Nostrand Reinhold Company
A Division of Litton Educational Publishing, Inc.
450 West 33rd Street, New York, N.Y. 10001

16 15 14 13 12 11 10 9 8 7 6 5 4 3 2 1

Library of Congress Cataloging in Publication Data

Illes, Robert E
    Men in stitches.

    1. Embroidery. 2. Needlework. 3. Punched work.
I. Title.
TT840.I42   746.4'4   74-22512
ISBN 0-442-23630-1

Acknowledgments

There is no way this book could have made it without the effort of the following people. The short phrases used after their names are no indication of the continual selfless and good-natured aid that most of them gave over a 4-year period. I am fortunate for their appearance on my scene, and I thank them more than they'll ever know: Dorothy Kizer, who started me on the correct way to punch; Richard Kizer, whose original ideas helped me to develop stands and frames — to say nothing of procuring materials for me at the oddest times; Jack Skelley, who first suggested this book, introduced me to Van Nostrand Reinhold, and helped during the gestation period; Florence Hickman, a teacher and weaver who taught me about color theory; Ken Arthur, an architect and artist who helped so much with visual presentations and pictures; John Messina and George H. Thompson of Color Labs, who supplied beautiful color photography and instant photo processing; Marie Loos, who drew the lovely art for the lettering diagrams; Warren and Tony Bredlow, whose hours of unstinting labor in making drawings, retouching photos, and keeping a dry crying-towel handy kept me alive; Dr. Rodney Mitchell, dentist and an artist in his own right, who helped me develop the hypodermic needle, without which there wouldn't be much to tell; Sue John McLeod, my favorite mother-in-law, who worked under heavy going in London to clear heraldic problems and obtain reproductions from the Victoria and Albert Museum; my son, Nick Illes, whose body, hands, and blithe spirit spent hours upon hot, cramped hours under photo lights for many of the illustrations; my charming wife Billie, who suffered the lonely hours and the cussing and capped it all with a superb job of preening and correcting the script, along with technical aid in weaving and encouragement at all hours, complete with meals; the delightful young ladies of Van Nostrand Reinhold Company — Nancy Newman, who put up with the idiocies of a first-time author; Barbara Klinger, who arranged the format of the tale; and Wendy Lochner (the wheel that turned!), with whom I had so much valuable and entertaining conversation; and Warner-Lambert Laboratories, who invented Rolaids.

Contents

TV Sports and Stitchery

When you take up stitchery, you can still log plenty of TV-sportcast time. What you are doing is *something* while the guys out on the field *ain't!* It's a lead-pipe cinch that what's cooking at the old ball game won't interfere with your doings. Really now, what is there to see while a pitcher looks at his shoes, kicks in the dirt, inspects his cleats, looks at first base, checks left field, cases the hot number in the third row, looks at his fingers, spits in his mitt, wonders why miniskirts went out of style, pulls down his cap, adjusts his scrotum, leans over, looks at the catcher, shakes his head, nods his head, stands up, bosoms the ball, and gets set to pitch — just in time for the batter to step out of the batter's box, spit on *his* hands, kick around in *his* dirt, pull on *his* cap, sneak a look at the third-row cutie, lean over, pick up dirt, hate pantsuits, get the stickum bag, step up to the plate, adjust *his* scrotum, wave his bat, glare at the pitcher, stand there, and watch a strike go whistling by? (And this scorching drama doesn't happen once but an average of 275 times per game!)

This whole tango has consumed 20 to 24 seconds, while it only takes 2 seconds to put the ball over the plate. You don't have to worry that you are about to miss anything if you continue to stitch through all this choreography, because, even if you didn't know what that guy on the little hill was doing out there, the announcer will holler like it was Lady Godiva, "Here comes the pitch!" And regardless of all that guff about change-ups and screwballs and curves and sliders — well, hell, they all look alike on a 17-inch screen.

If a guy gets a hit, you'll know about it, what with all the screaming and hollering — it is such a fortuitous break in the tedium.

One baseball season I made a whole hook rug — 130,000 hooks of it. During that time I compiled some very interesting statistics. I found that the number of hooks I could make between each pitch averaged out at 5; for each foul ball, 7; for each single, 8; for each double (replayed twice), 12; for each walk, 14; for each home run (replayed once), 14; for each mound conference (that's where the manager comes out and asks the pitcher if he has noticed that hot chick in the third row), 18; for each change of pitchers, 28 — plus a run at the icebox for a cold beer. No wonder baseball's in trouble. It's more exciting to watch your toenails grow. And to call it the National Pastime! All men know that girl watching is their National Pastime, and all girls know that *their* National Pastime is fixing up to get and getting watched.

Speaking of girl watching, college football has it all over baseball — when things bog down, those TV guys up and down the sidelines zero in on all those good-looking, straight-toothed, tight-bosomed coeds. (Notice how fast those gals sense they're on TV? Innate, man, innate.) That's when you better stop punching, or you'll run a needle clear up your arm and knit yourself into the rug. (Can't you just hear it? "Charley needs vacuuming today.")

Where you really hit the licks in your punching during football is on the replays — in slow motion with all those dreamlike human balloons floating around. It's a good thing their grunts aren't in slow motion; they'd sound like enamored hippos in rutting time. Often there is so much instant replay that they miss the whole next play and have to show a replay of the one they missed while they were showing the first one. Every now and then some nice advertiser will buy some time and let the TV guys get caught up.

But some of those ads! "Official time-out," they call it. Boy! I'd hate to see some "unofficial-time-out" ads. I don't have to hear about a Chevrolet keeping the USA on the track every six minutes — I can't even afford one every six *years!* And how about that moose or whatever it is running all over the place selling insurance? Who ever heard of buying insurance from a *moose?*

What really rips me off is when half-time comes along, and they start trotting out all those pretty little band girls in the teeny-weeny pants. Damn if they don't take up the whole half showing replays — at least they could show regirls! They've got them on tape, too.

I'm telling you, if you learn how to *listen* to TV, in a season or two you can end up with wall-to-wall rugs all over your house. Or even some floor-to-ceiling rugs. Which in some quarters are called padded cells.

1

What is a Stitch?

"In sewing," answers Noah Webster, "it is a single pass of the needle, or the loop, or the turn of the thread." If you had never seen a stitch, do you think you could make one from that? A stitch, he also says, is "a local and sudden pain." Maybe you didn't pass the needle right?

Now the "needle" in Noah's definition comes off as, "a small instrument for sewing, sharp at one end, with a hole for a thread." He doesn't say where the hole is; he doesn't say what shape the instrument is. With one of the outstandingly brilliant statements of all time, Noah gets it all together in his definition of "needle-work" as — hold on to your chair — "work with a needle"!

This book is about "needlework," all right, but instead of discussing stitchery using the common little, solid, steel rods, sharply pointed at one end with a hole for thread in the other end, it deals with *punch stitchery.* You will be using not only the usual rug-punching needle, a hollow, metal shaft with a hole for thread or yarn at the pointed end, but also such an unlikely character as the hypodermic needle, which provides a smaller, finer stitch.

Now there is no big mystery about what a stitch is. All of us have stood at our mother's knee while she whipped the needle back and forth making some strategic repairs, like replacing those buttons that held our pants up. All that was ordinary stitching. Those same stitches used in upholding our dignity could just as well have been sewed onto the surface of a cloth for decoration, in which case they would be "embroidery."

In fact, throughout history, from the dim mists of antiquity to our brightly lit present, man has always done decorative needlework. From the lake dwellers of prehistoric Switzerland, who sewed clothes with slivered bones for needles and linen for thread, down to the pad renters of today, people have expressed themselves with *acu pingere,* a term used by Virgil for "painting with a needle." Pieces of cloth embroidery remain from the tomb of Amenhotep, 1500 B.C., and from the civilizations of Babylon and Persia. There are descriptions in The Book of Exodus of the robes of Aaron (28), the hangings in the Tabernacle (26), and the "broideries" relating to the prophecies of Ezekiel (27). There are the wonders of Byzantine stitchery and the French, German, and Spanish schools of yore; to-day, there is also the breathtaking beauty of the machine-embroidered, synthetic place mats of Woolworth's. Through all time, man has had the urge to embellish the surface of a fabric by sticking something through it.

This work in ancient Greece was called variegation. In Babylonia, it was called by the name of the color used, such as bluework and redwork. In the Middle Ages, embroidery was called by the name of the piece it was applied to, such as mantlework or capework. In that Age of Chivalry, when all the ladies had to do was to sit in their drafty castles and sew while waiting for their tin-suited swains to return from their interminable wars, another name for needlework could have been boredom. By whatever name and with whatever tool, needlework implies the decoration by means of a needle of finished, woven material.

There are differences among the various types of needlework, however. In free-style embroidery, as in ordinary stitching, a rod-type needle — with the eye *opposite* the pointed end — is used to draw strands of cotton thread or silk, wool, or synthetic yarn back and forth through the fabric, thereby placing the thread or yarn alternately on the front and rear of the cloth. The aim is to arrange the stitches on the front of the cloth so that they form a design. To achieve this goal, the needle may be inserted anywhere through the front or rear surface, and the thread may cover whatever area is deemed desirable. The result is that the decorative stitches that appear so prettily on one side of the material can leave the other side a rather messy affair.

In needlepoint and other counted-thread embroidery, also done with a rod-type needle, the stitches are again arranged to form a design on the front of the material, but here the weave of the material determines the exact placement of the stiches, because the needle must be inserted in the holes formed by the crossing of the horizontal (weft) and vertical (warp) threads. The design, therefore, must generally conform to the geometric nature of the woven fabric. Again, the needle is drawn back and forth through the material, being inserted in one hole and withdrawn from another, and the decorative thread or yarn appears alternately on the front and rear of the background cloth.

Punch stitchery is an entirely different matter. For one thing, a hollow needle, whose thread-bearing hole is at the *pointed* end, is used. For another, the needle is inserted into the *front surface* of the fabric only. It is pushed in between the weft and warp threads just far enough to deposit a short length of thread, which hangs down from the rear surface. When the needle is then pulled up and withdrawn from the same hole, it leaves behind a length of thread in the form of a loop, which protrudes from the rear surface. The needle is then moved along the front surface of the background fabric to the next point of insertion, which places a length of thread on the front surface of the material, and your second punch stitch is made.

The second punch stitch secures the length of thread to the front of the fabric and forms a second loop on the rear of it. With each subsequent punch, a decorative length of thread is left lying flat on the front surface of the cloth, between every two insertions, and a loop is left protruding from the rear of the cloth. This means that either side of the cloth can become the decorative one if care is taken to assure uniform loops.

I don't mean that you can hang the completed punchwork on the wall for a while and then flip it over to the reverse side and walk on it. The side of the work that will ultimately be used has to be planned and the plan followed, because flipping the work over reverses the design: a landscape showing a low, morning sun, if it is flipped over, will become a sunset. I do mean that the same process can be used for making two different types of usable surfaces: the looped side for rugs or textural wall hangings and the flat side for a design similar to needlepoint work or free embroidery.

When the looped side is to appear as the completed work, the uniformity of the loops can be assured by setting a gauge on the needle, thereby preventing the shaft from penetrating further into the cloth than the desired distance, like the depth gauge on a drill. Basically, the procedure is to fill the back side of the background cloth with loops by punch stitching into the front of it. The loops are held in place by the friction between the cloth and the inserted yarn. The design is controlled by the placement of the flat stitches on the front or working surface of the cloth. The length of each flat stitch (the space between two punches) is usually from ⅜ to ½ inch to assure a closely packed appearance on the looped side. As packing proceeds, the loops have a tendency to become entangled, and the colors on the loop side must be separated to maintain the design. That is all there really is to the whole process.

When the front of the cloth is to be the completed side, several different effects can be obtained. First of all, there is a purely linear effect, which is used to stitch the undulating coastlines and finely lettered names on map designs (see Chapter 7). The punch stitches merely follow the outlines of the design.

On the other hand, there are designs in which solid areas of stitchery are desired. In those cases, the flat stitches can be arranged to give the studied effect of needlepoint by punching the stitches into the holes in straight rows at a 45-degree angle to the straight lines of the threads. Punching in diagonal rows is necessary to maintain correct tension and to keep the stitches full and uniform. When stitches are punched in horizontal or vertical rows along the thread lines, the extra pressure required to force the stitches into place tends to pull the yarn taut, resulting in a thin, hard line that does not fully cover the area. Several such rows give a striated effect with stripes of background cloth showing through. When it is absolutely necessary to punch a stitch or row of stitches parallel to a warp or weft thread line — in order to follow a curve in the design, for instance — the entry hole should be spread with the needle to ease the tension by inserting the beveled surface of the needle point at a 45-degree angle in relation to the vertical or horizontal threads of the background.

In addition to the uniform, needlepoint effect, solid coverage can be worked to show various textures, such as velour, fur, or feathers, by punching the stitches in varying lengths with a more random placement. With this technique, if the needle is occasionally pushed into a weft or warp thread instead of into the interstices between them, it will not harm the overall effect, so punching need not be as precise, that is, into the holes, as is necessary to achieve the needlepoint effect. Whenever the flat stitches form the design side, it is wise to allow the loops at the back of the cloth to remain entangled as an aid in securing the stitches.

Before I get carried away, it is a good idea to go over the kinds of materials and equipment you will be using and how you will be using them. This will give you a better idea of what I am talking about.

2

The Materials

As with other forms of stitching, the size of the needle, the weave of the cloth, and the thickness of the thread or yarn are all interrelated. Basically, the thread or yarn should correspond as closely as possible to the diameter of the needle being used; the needle size, in turn, is chosen according to the fineness or coarseness of the background cloth. The more threads there are to the inch, the finer the weave of the cloth, which requires a thinner needle and correspondingly thinner thread. As a rough guide, you will be using a large rug-punch needle (Columbia-Minerva) with heavy yarn on 13- to 15-count cotton cloth, a medium-size punch needle (Boye No. 2) with six strands of embroidery thread on 20- to 26-count cloth, and a 16-gauge hypo-punch needle with three strands of embroidery thread on 22- to 28-count linen (Figure 2-1). If you are really ambitious, you can use a 20-gauge hypo needle with one strand of embroidery thread on 42-count linen.

NEEDLES

You will have needles of several different sizes and types. Get yourself two covered boxes: one for your large punch needles and one for your smaller punch needles. For your regular sewing needles, use a box designed to hold 3-by-5-inch filing cards. The file box can be separated into different compartments to store the needles in marked envelopes according to size, and each divider can be used to record the purpose the needle was used for, where, and the size of thread.

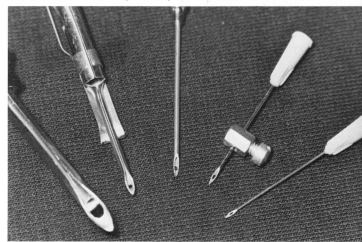

2-1. The recommended needles, from left to right: Columbia-Minerva rug needle, Boye punch needle, and 16-, 18-, and 20-gauge hypo needles.

PUNCH NEEDLES

You can get regular punch needles at any hobby or knit shop and in some needlework shops, although needlework shops sort of disdain rug makers. Get the Columbia-Minerva Deluxe Rug Needle Set, which comes with a hollow handle and two interchangeable points. You will use the larger No. 2 point more often for the rug business and the No. 0 point for more delicate, wall-hanging work. Because the yarn is threaded through the handle of the Columbia-Minerva needle, there is less likelihood of hangups and snagging than with other needles of this type. The upper part of the handle is notched to adjust the length of the loops, which allows you to control the uniformity of the depth of the pile. As the adjustment gizmo will damage your hand in time and also become disengaged in the heat of creation, allowing the loop control to slip, I wrap a Band-Aid around the notched adjuster lock.

A smaller needle is the No. 2 Boye Punch Needle. This is a great needle for punching six-strand embroidery thread. It, too, has a guide for controlling the depth of the punches, but this one is tame and needs no taping. I used this needle to make the maps of the British Isles and Europe shown in Figures C-7 and C-5. The one problem with the Boye needle is that it is split down one side for loading thread. This slit, I found, snagged the embroidery thread. To overcome this, cut a small piece of Mystik tape and press it over the slot at the top (flat) end of the needle (Figure 2-2). Then insert the end of a tweezer into the needle to press the tape onto the inside surface (Figure 2-3). This will allow embroidery thread to slip through the needle without snagging. To load the needle with this end closed, moisten the thread in your mouth enough to increase its weight and make it pointed and drop it into the back of the needle. With a few slings, like shaking down a thermometer, the thead will be impelled down the length of the needle and out of the end. The thread can then be pulled through the hole at the pointed end, passing it through the beveled surface of the point to the rear. As mouth chemistry can change the color permanently, cut off the wet, darkened portion before starting to punch.

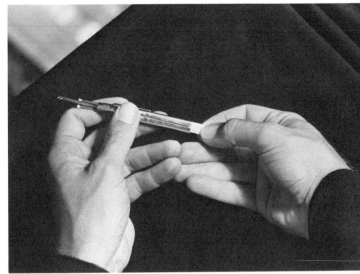

2-2.

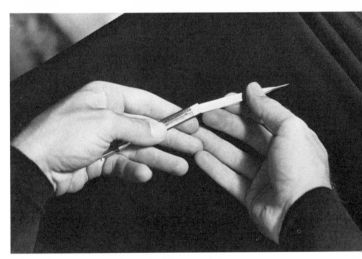

2-3.

ROD-TYPE NEEDLES

In addition to these punch needles, you will need some rod-type needles. The most indispensable of these are beading needles, which are used for fine map lettering and for threading hypodermic needles. They are made by Walco and Boye. You should have four or five packages of these needles, as they are hard to hold and will become bent with use. For threading these fine needles, a gizmo called a *push threader* is available, which saves eyesight and patience. A package of two or three can usually be purchased at notions counters, but, like a lot of things we take for granted, they are sometimes scarce.

For experimentation, you can get an inexpensive assortment of rod-type needles. A package of fifty put out by Boye includes long and short needles for tapestry, yarn, and cotton; sharp-pointed needles; and something called betweens, which are sort of mongrels. Keep the assorted needles and beading needles in marked envelopes in the card box with notes listing what size and color thread you used with each size and type of needle. This is especially important for projects containing lettering, because you will want to duplicate portions of the lettering, and the card-box record will save a lot of bothersome reexperimentation.

HYPODERMIC NEEDLES

Finally, we come to the high point of our needle selection, which is the hypodermic needle. A punch needle made from a hypodermic needle is exactly like any other punch needle, except that it is very small. This enables you to make very fine stitches, using from one to three strands of six-strand embroidery thread.

Unfortunately, it is not so easy to obtain this needle. You would think that your family doctor, who has been privy not only to all of the internal gurglings of your body but also to your most fanciful flights of mind for twenty years or so, would not exhibit such consternation at a request for a hypodermic needle. It just goes to show that no man knows how he is looked upon by his fellow man. When I asked my doctor for a hypo needle, he became very evasive, and when I explained that I wanted it to stitch with, he began edging toward the nearest exit. He had seen too many late, late movies. In contrast to his treatment — one of the few I wasn't billed for — I was surprised to find that I could buy the needles at the local drugstore by the gross, no questions asked. What is true in one part of the country is not necessarily true elsewhere, however, so check into the legality of such sales in your own region before visiting your drugstore.

Once the hypo needle has been obtained, the next problem is to drill a hole through the bevel at the pointed end. The only person with whom you may be acquainted who is equipped to drill such a hole is the same person who, whether you like it or not, drills most of the other new holes you acquire — your friendly dentist. If you have ever had a filling, you know that he is a good source for hypo needles.

Using a drill head called a one-half round burr, my dentist drilled the required holes in 16-, 18-, and 20-gauge needles at the amazing speed of 250,000 revolutions per minute. To start each hole, he used a diamond-pointed bit. The hole was then lengthened into an elliptical slot running up and down the side opposite the bevel of the needle, as in any rug-punch needle, by using the one-half round burr. The length of the slot in the 16-gauge needle was one and one-half times the diameter of the burr. In the 18- and 20-gauge needles, the length of the slot was just equal to the diameter of the burr, or round. While he is hot with the drill, have him do several needles of each size in case you lose one or he goofs.

Dentists have the cutest names for those little gadgets that can create such havoc in your psyche and bring on such palpitations of fear. Instead of rational names like grinder or drill, they hang on names such as Dedico, friction gripstone, and midget-sized burlew fulci! That last one sounds like it ought to have feathers on it and chirp, but it is only a pumice wheel. These tools come in handy, however, especially if you intend to keep on using your own teeth.

To eliminate microscopic filings, which may adhere to the holes in the needles after drilling and which would snag the thread and make the needles useless, my friendly dentist first buffed the holes with a white friction gripstone (a fine-grained conical drill with pumice and synthetic-rubber fibers), then polished them off with a friction-grip white Dedico (a pumice-impregnated rubber buffing wheel) — both at low speeds so as not to scorch and soften the stainless steel. Your friendly Dedico driver can do this in a trice.

The outer, elliptical edge of the needle's point is razor-sharp, and it should also be buffed so that it won't shear the cloth into which it is punched. This can be done by hand, using a cuttlefish disk (which your dentist can give you), pumice, or a similar polishing stone. Carefully stroke the stone along the outer edges of the bevel until they feel smooth when tested with a sideways motion of the fingers, like testing the sharpness of a knife with your thumb. Try sticking the needle into a piece of taut silk. If the point splits a filament or if the sides of the bevel leave a frayed appearance in the silk, round off the point and buff the bevel a bit more with the cuttlefish disk. *Do not dull the edges!* Round them off until the needle will separate the filaments but won't split them; the needle will then slide into the cloth without shearing it.

LOADING THE NEEDLES

Let's tackle the tiny hypodermic needle first.

1. Since the shaft is so narrow, the thread will have to be drawn through the hole with the help of a fine beading needle made of steel and a magnet. To see if the beading needle is truly steel (almost all of them are), test it with the magnet. If the needle sticks, it is steel. If it doesn't, it is some sort of alloy, probably stainless steel, and it won't do. Similarly, the hypo needle must be stainless steel (again, almost all of them are) so that it does not interfere with the magnetic pull on the beading needle. You are going to use the rod needle with a loop of thread to pull the decorative thread down through the hollow shaft of the hypo needle. To check that the rod needle is the proper size to go through the hypo, drop the former down through the latter. If it won't slip through unassisted without a thread loop, it certainly won't go through with a thread loop and three strands of embroidery thread tagging along. Try a thinner beading needle.

2. The next step is to thread the steel rod needle with extrafine *cotton* thread, forming a loop about 3 inches in length. Tie the two thread ends together with an overhand knot, pull the knot tight, and clip the surplus thread ends off (Figure 2-4).

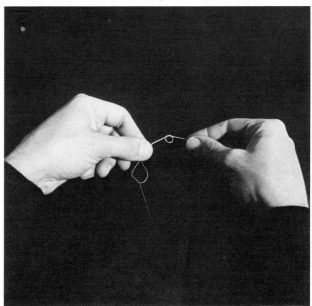

2-4.

3. Move the knot so that it is equidistant from the point and the eye of the needle. Make the loop at the needle's eye as sharp as possible by moistening it and pinching it into an elongated shape. Cotton thread is essential for the loop, because synthetic or silk sewing thread cannot be dampened and shaped.

4. If you are using a 16-gauge hypo and three strands of embroidery thread (use a size-7 milliner's needle for the loop), you *may* first insert the decorative thread into the loop prior to dropping the rod needle through the back of the hypo (Figure 2-5). The weight of the milliner's needle may cause it to drop through the hypo without the aid of a magnet. Hold the hypo needle vertically in one hand, with the point directed downward, and hold the decorative thread, with the loop and needle dangling from it, in the other hand. Drop the steel needle down through the top of the hypo needle until it stops of its own accord (Figure 2-6). To pull the steel needle through the rest of the way, stroke down the length of the hypo needle with the magnet from the top of the shaft toward the point (Figure 2-7). The first stroke should pull the steel needle through. If it doesn't, repeat the stroking motion with the magnet. If the steel needle persists in not slipping through the hypo, remoisten and resqueeze the cotton thread to narrow its shape at the eye of the steel needle and make sure that the knot is still at half-mast along the needle. Drop the steel needle back into the shaft and try the magnet again.

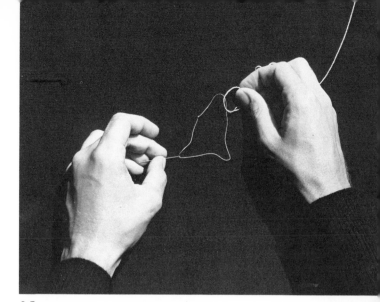

2-5.

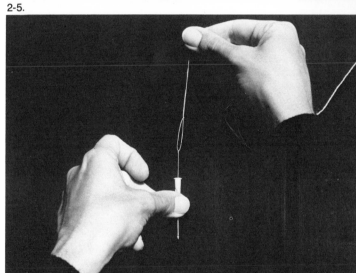

2-6.

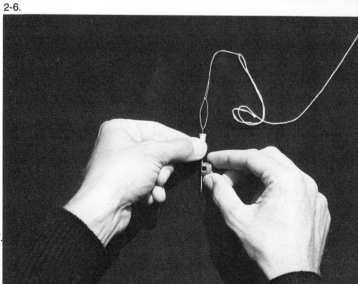

2-7.

5. In case you want to use a 20-gauge hypo needle for one strand of embroidery thread, use a beading needle for the thread loop. First, insert the rod needle with its loop into the hypo and pull it through with the magnet, leaving a portion of the thread loop above the end of the hypo. The clearance of the beading needle through the 20-gauge hypo is so slight that, with a thread loop, even if it is pinched sharp, it will never slip through without a magnetic stroke or two. *Then* insert the decorative thread into the loop portion above the hypo's end and pull it through. The reason: it is easier to use the magnet with only the thread loop when you are using one strand of embroidery thread than to have the one decorative strand, somewhat indistinguishable from the loop and filled with diabolical quirks, getting tangled up among your fingers, falling around, or trussing up the cat if you have one. To aid in distinguishing the loop from the decorative thread, I suggest that you use black or white thread for the loop.

6. Once the point of the steel needle is protruding from the business end of the hypo, you need only pull the steel needle to bring the cotton loop bearing the decorative thread completely through the hypo shaft (Figure 2-8). Pull a generous length of decorative thread through the shaft; then remove the loop and steel needle and store them for future use. (They can be attached to a convenient object, such as a metal lamp, with the magnet. If you happen to lose the loop needle, just go barefoot — you'll find it quickly enough!)

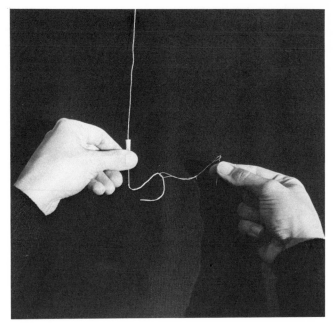

2-8.

7. You now have the decorative thread through the hypo shaft and can proceed to insert it into the slotted eye, pushing it in from the beveled face of the point and drawing it out from the curved, rear surface (Figure 2-9). Pull just enough of the decorative thread back up through the top of the hypo so that about ¾ inch remains inserted through the eye (Figure 2-10).

8. To stitch, place a forefinger over the top of the needle and insert the point into the cloth so that the loose end of thread emerges underneath the cloth (Figure 2-11). Withdraw the needle, while holding the thread end dangling from the underneath surface with your forefinger and thumb. Reinsert the needle through the cloth a minute space away from the first poke and you have made your first stitch. Olé!

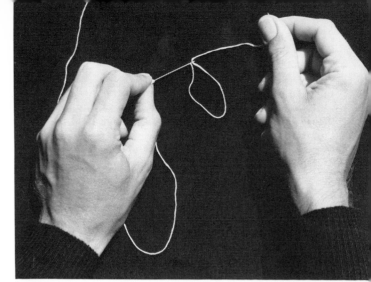

2-9.

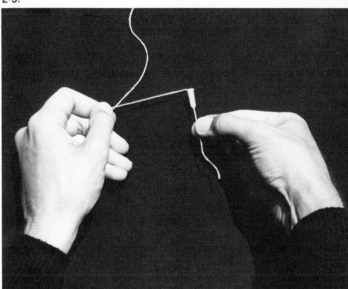

2-10.

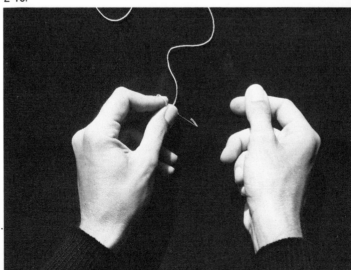

2-11.

More about stitching later. Now, let's describe how to load the Columbia-Minerva rug needle.

    1. If you have ever tried to get yarn down one of these "easy-to-load" needles, you are familiar with frustration. To overcome this, buy from your hobby shop a 2-foot length of piano wire and bend it in the middle to form a rather sharply pointed loop that is narrow enough to slip easily through the tube of the rug needle (Figure 2-12).

    2. Hold the rug needle with the point directed down toward your wrist, hara-kiri position, and slip the wire loop up into the shaft, starting at the point of the needle. Push it up from the pointed end all the way to the back of the needle until 1 or 2 inches of the wire loop stick out the back opening of the needle (Figure 2-13).

    3. Thread about 2 inches of your yarn through the wire loop and pull the wire back down the shaft until it emerges with the yarn at the pointed end of the needle (Figure 2-14).

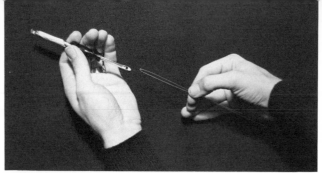

2-12.

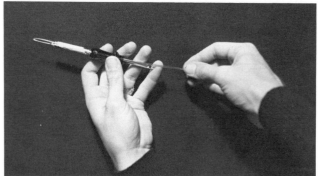

2-13.

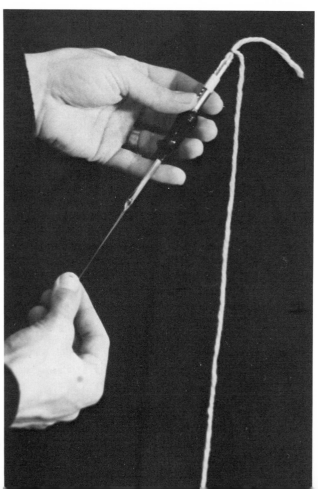

2-14.

22

4. Stick the two-pronged end of the wire loop through the needle's eye, inserting it from the beveled side, and pull it through to the flat side (Figure 2-15). If you have managed to keep the yarn in the tip of the wire loop during these simple little maneuvers, you have loaded your rug needle (Figure 2-16). After you have reduced the amount of yarn hanging out of the tip of the needle so that only 1 inch dangles, you are off to the races.

Since these thin, wire loops are shy little beasts, they will manage to slip away and hide from you. So that you can more easily follow their spoor, I suggest that you dip the two-pronged ends into some red nail polish, which will make them easier to spot on the floor, where they like to domicile.

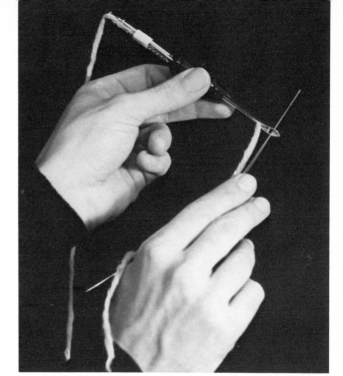

2-15.

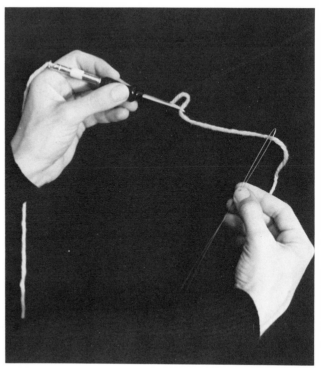

2-16.

CLOTH

When man first stuck his head out of his cave at the end of the Ice Age, he found that he had a clothing problem. The ensuing competition for pelts, between the wearer and the wearee, lasted for eons. In time, man found it simpler and safer to plant seeds for fiber and to mat or weave the fibers into cloth than to chase after his next suit of clothes with a mean animal inside it.

All you need to know about weaving for your purposes, beyond cutting down a little on the juice, is that a series of vertical threads — the warp — forms the foundation of the cloth and is crossed — alternately intertwined — with a series of horizontal threads — the weft. It is called filling the foundation, which is not quite the same as a provocative postern oscillating down the avenue in a tight girdle. When the individual warp threads are regularly interlaced with the individual weft threads in the above fashion, the construction is called a *tabby weave*. This is the preferred construction for our background fabrics. In addition, when there are an equal number of warp and weft threads per square inch, it is called a *square count*. The number of threads per square inch can vary from thirteen for coarse material to forty-two for exceptionally fine material. Two cloths that are particularly recommended for punch stitchery are monk's cloth and tabby linen.

MONK'S CLOTH

With the rise of the religious orders and monasteries during the period called the Dark Ages, the cloth woven by monks in their self-sufficient abbeys became known as *monk's cloth*. As the quality of this cloth was upgraded, its name was subsequently promoted to abbot's cloth and even bishop's cloth. This commodity, made from the better fibers available only to the monks, became so important in England in medieval times that a monk's cloth became a unit of measure for a worsted fabric 12 yards long and 45 inches wide. At a much later date, this cloth acquired other names, selected to maintain a patina of antiquity, such as friar's cloth, druid's cloth, cloister cloth, and mission cloth. In the beginning, all such cloth was made of homespun wool. Nowadays, it is manufactured primarily of cotton.

Monk's cloth is a doubled variation of the plain tabby weave. Instead of interlacing individual threads, two adjacent warp threads are crossed as a unit by two weft threads. The pattern formed by crossing successive pairs of warp threads is more apparent than that made by crossing single threads; the resulting construction is called a *basket weave*. Since the adjacent threads are worked in pairs, this cloth is also known as a *two-by-two square count*. The regular basket weave can also be worked on a three-by-three or four-by-four thread pattern, but for ease in stenciling and punching a design, the two-by-two weave is best.

There are as many different types of monk's cloth as there are companies making it. In fact, some companies make more than one grade. It is very important that all four threads used in the weave of the cloth you buy are the same weight and thickness and are somewhat heavy, although soft and twinelike in appearance (Figure 2-17). A lightweight monk's cloth is not suitable for wall hangings, as it sags so much that it would take an elaborate latticework frame to hold it up. A proper monk's cloth for punching should be a rather soft, bulky material that is woven close enough for the interlocked threads not to slither and slip around. Do not get a monk's cloth that has weft threads of a lighter, thinner caliber than the warp threads, or vice versa (Figure 2-18).

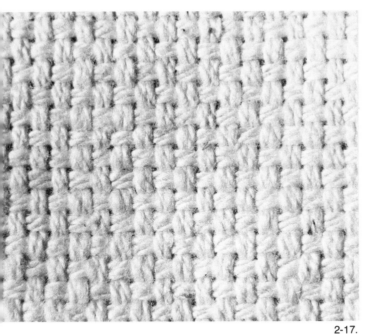

2-17.

2-18.

The monk's cloth that I have found best for rugs or hangings is woven by Southern Mills. The monk's cloth by Cannon, although excellent for drapes, furniture coverings, and other nonstitching crafts, is of a heavy warp and light weft construction, which is plain murder to make a rug with. I ought to know. I chased the design of the Tree Rug (see Figure C-9) on it for over a quarter of a million stitches.

Paradoxically, monk's cloth is both nonstretching and resilient. When it is tacked to a frame, it can be pulled wider at the expense of its length or longer at the expense of its width, but it will not stretch to an increase of total area. Once tension has been released, the cloth will reform to its original size. That is, it will reform if no great amount of yarn has been inserted into it. I have found that when yarn has been inserted, monk's cloth tends to "draw up." Therefore, when the dimensions of a completed project must be accurate, as for a wall-to-wall rug, after the design has been completely filled with yarn, the cloth should be relaxed from all tension and remeasured. Chances are that it will have drawn up along one of its dimensions. If so, additional stitches will have to be made along the shorter dimension, filling in some of the extra material left as a safety border around the design.

Monk's cloth is not the easiest stuff to find. Upholstery or wholesale fabric outlets are the most likely sources. Hobby shops occasionally carry it, although you may have to buy cloth that has already been printed with a pattern. You can turn this over and use the unprinted side. Always make sure that you buy a piece big enough to have plenty of border beyond your design — you can always cut it off after your project is done. Splicing monk's cloth to get a large enough area will make old sailors cry.

This cloth can be punched and pummeled with needles and vehemence without detriment. It's a great whipping boy for your frustrations and resentments. You can't hurt it, and it's a lot cheaper than your friendly psychiatrist. Why not tell him about it — he has frustrations and resentments, too.

LINEN

It is hard to guess how the complex methods of changing flax to linen evolved; the process was old by the time of Genesis and Exodus (41:42 and 9:31, respectively). The method involves beating flax stems on sharp spikes attached to a board to separate the fibers from the woody rind. The stalks are whacked down onto the spikes and given a short pull. The number of spikes per square inch is increased for each subsequent beating, which separates the flax into finer and finer shreds. The spikes, like what happens to Fido's back when he is riled, are called hackles, and the whacking process is called heckling, which helps to explain dogs and politicians.

The fibers are spun into strands of thread, which are then woven into cloth. I find that tabby linen with a one-by-one construction is the most suitable background cloth for fine work (Figure 2-19). *One-by-one* indicates that each warp thread is crossed by a weft thread in the regular over-and-under pattern of the tabby weave. A one-by-one tabby, regardless of the count or the thickness of the warp and weft threads, is uniform, creating a reliable system of squares for lettering map projects — for maintaining uniformity of height, width, and spacing among the letters. This linen, especially the square count, is stiff enough to support the lettering and keep it from roving and sagging.

Linen is easy to trace a design onto, as the tops of the interwoven threads are flat. However, once a tracing mark has been made, it can hardly be eradicated, because linen is sized. The tracing is literally on the sizing and not the linen, and any attempt to wash a spot away will melt the sizing, carrying an off-colored mess into neighboring fibers. If this event occurs, the way to overcome it is to start over.

Linen can have at most three insertions of thread in any one spot, meaning that you are entitled to make only two mistakes requiring removal of the same stitch. The third time has to be the charm, because linen, with its sizing, tends to grab embroidery thread. Pulling out an inserted thread for the third time will cause the linen to separate, split, and break.

The best place for buying linen at reasonable prices is a needlework shop, where remnants — pieces not really large enough for most projects — may be lying around waiting for someone to give them a home. Fabric-remnant shops are not necessarily bargain centers, and they are not necessarily remnant shops either. Bear in mind that good, heavy-weave, plain linen in white or off-white can run into quite a few dollars a yard. You should be able to get irregular pieces large enough for two or more projects in needlework shops for much less.

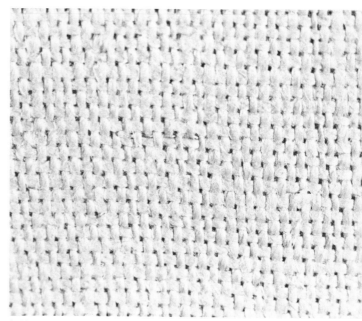

2-19.

26

YARNS AND THREADS

As you might suppose, the spinning of yarn and thread has as illustrious a history as the making of cloth. You have only to catch a glimpse of the handspinner in action to admire the ingenuity of the process, drawing out thick fibers into thin ones and twisting short fibers together to join them into one long, continuous strand. High in the Peruvian Andes, near Cuzco, I saw a woman sitting on a stone near the ancient pre-Inca fortress of Sacsahuaman, spinning alpaca thread with only her hands. About 50 feet away, held to the ground by a rock, was the end, or beginning, of her thread. Reaching into a sling over her shoulder, she would get a small pinch of alpaca fur and, with a motion like sprinkling salt, rub the fur back and forth in her fingers, adding it onto the end of the thread in her hands, and then back further away as her thread grew longer. The only sound was that of the moaning wind through the mysterious and monolithic stones of the ancient fortress.

I have also seen, in a textile factory in New Jersey, a room so long that it vanished to a point, its entire length filled with row upon row of screaming machinery, all carding floss and spinning thread by the millions of yards per day. And the only sound was that of a tornado. From Rumplestiltskin to Burlington Mills, man has continually made thread.

RUG YARN

There are many different yarns available. What we are interested in are rug yarns — thick, bulky yarns — as opposed to the thinner knitting yarns (four-ply sports or worsteds) and embroidery yarns (crewel, tapestry, and Persian wool, for instance). Rug yarns that formerly were all-cotton are now a combination of cotton and synthetic fibers — and they are just great! They punch and fill monk's cloth well. They are lighter in weight, brighter in color, and they don't mat or crush as 100-percent-cotton yarns do. They are easier to clean and accept Scotchguarding well.

If you find that these yarns do not suit your idea of color, you can use wool rug yarn. The eye of the Bird Rug (Figure C-10) is wool. Wool is very compressible, however, and when it is used along with the synthetic-cotton blend, it will have to be inserted densely enough to stand up against the heavier yarn next to it, or it will be overlapped and covered. Therefore, the wool stitches should be closer together, so two or three times as many as usual can be packed into the area.

Yarns come in loosely coiled skeins and can be purchased all over the place: department stores, fabric shops, knit shops, hobby shops, variety stores, or five-and-ten-cents (make that one-and-two-dollars) stores. The big problem is finding enough yarn of the same dye lot.

A *dye lot* is an amount of yarn or thread that has been dyed with the same color in the same pot at the same time. Each time a lot is dyed, it is given a separate number, which is called the *dye-lot number*. It is almost always true that, if you buy the same manufacturers' dye-lot number, even from different shops, you will end up with the same color. But it *is* possible to have a variance of color within one and the same dye lot.

To check the color of the yarn, do not look at it under fluorescent light, which kills color. To get the true reflection of the yarn, view the looped ends of the skein in daylight; when you are buying several skeins from a loose display, view all the skeins together in the same manner. The looped ends reflect less light than the long sides of a skein and appear darker in color. As you will be looking at the loops in a rug, looking at the bunched ends of a skein is a more accurate way to choose your colors.

To figure the number of skeins of any one color that will be necessary in your project, first figure, as closely as possible, the number of square inches that are to be covered by that color. Do this roughly if it is a large project. If it's a small area, you are going to buy the whole skein anyhow.

Mark off, on a sample piece of cloth of the type you are going to use for your project, a specific number of square inches, for example, 4 inches by 4 inches. Using a sample of yarn intended for your project, fill in the predetermined number of square inches of space with the yarn.

The amount of yarn used will vary as the closeness of one punch to another varies. The more punches you make per square inch, the more yarn it will take per square inch. Also, the length of the loop you wish to walk on or see hanging on the wall will affect the amount of yarn used. When you are satisfied with the density and the length of the stitches and have filled the measured area, cut the yarn. For future reference, make a note of how deep the needle was inserted to obtain the specified loop length.

Finally, pull all the trial yarn out of the cloth and measure its length. Now you will know how many feet of yarn it took to fill a 4-inch-by-4-inch square. That will allow you to calculate the total number of yarn feet required for the total area to be covered. Divide this number by the number of feet in a single skein (this should be printed on the label) to determine how many skeins of the same color and dye lot you need.

Regardless of how accurate you consider your calculations to be, always add 25 percent to that number. This additional amount will replace any yarn you might discard due to improper color or stitching errors. Once yarn or embroidery thread has been inserted into cloth and then removed it should not be used again. The tension previously applied to it in stitching will thin its diameter, and this will show adversely in the finished work.

To prepare the skeins of yarn for use, they should be uncoiled and rolled into balls, which makes it easy to feed the yarn into the needle as work proceeds. Placing each ball of yarn in a plastic bag and attaching the bags with staples or thumb tacks to the top of your frame will avert a lot of trouble. As far as I know, there has never been any scientific investigation in the field of animal psychology that explains the magnetism between balls of yarn and kittens. The pussy-proof plastic bags will prevent your having to unhook your playful kitten, while still providing it with batting practice. To avoid self-impalement, however, avoid concurrent punching and pussy watching.

EMBROIDERY THREAD

While the term *yarn* generally implies that the original fibers or filaments have been more or less loosely twisted together to form the strand, *thread* indicates tightly twisted fibers or filaments, resulting in a finer, smoother strand. In both cases, two or more single strands, each called a *ply*, may be twisted together to form stronger yarns and threads. There are two-, four-, and eight-ply embroidery threads, which are sold under a multitude of names, such as pearl cotton, coton à broder, and soft embroidery. Many people also use various three- and four-ply crochet cottons as embroidery thread. However, the most commonly available and most useful embroidery thread is called stranded cotton or six-strand cotton, and it is sold in small skeins of about 8 yards. Stranded cotton is actually composed of six two-ply threads; each tightly twisted double-ply thread is considered as a single strand, and the six strands are twisted together loosely enough so that they may be separated into two-ply threads. This enables you to do finer work, using only three or even one of the six strands, and it allows you to mix strands of different shades to get gradations of color.

Separating the strands can be done the complicated way, the hopeless way, and the four-letter-word way. It can also be done the simple way. For this you will need two hooks affixed to a wall or a door and a space large enough to allow you to back up 6 or 8 feet away from them. Plastic suction hooks are probably the best choice, as they will not mar the surface to which they are attached.

1. Affix the two hooks to the wall or door at about your shoulder height and about 2 feet apart from each other. Grasp the skein of thread in your left hand, holding it by the two little paper sleeves wrapped around it, your forefinger over one and your little finger over the other. With your right hand, pick up the thread end sticking out of the inside of the skein and loop the thread over one hook (Figure 2-20).

2-20.

2. Now simply back up, pulling the coiled thread out of the skein into a simple, straight piece (Figure 2-21). You can unwind the entire skein or you can stop and clip the thread at any point in unraveling, leaving the unpulled portion in the sleeves and allowing the unraveled portion to fall on the floor. (If you unravel the entire skein, it is advisable, especially for shorter persons, to cut the resulting line of thread into two or three sections for greater ease in handling it.)

3. With thumb and forefinger of each hand, pick up the loose line of thread from the floor, holding your arms wide apart and raising them over your head so that the cut ends of the thread are off the floor and are able to spin freely (Figure 2-22). When this spinning has ceased, you now have a relaxed piece of thread.

2-21.

2-22.

4. Take one end and untwist about 2 inches of the intertwined strands, smoothing and flattening the strands so that they lie parallel to each other (Figure 2-23). It is now possible to separate the six strands into two groups by taking three adjacent strands in your left hand and three adjacent strands in your right hand and pulling them apart. It is almost always possible to tell which strands are adjacent to each other by smoothing out the twist first. In any case, it isn't hard to tell when you have gotten the wrong strands, because they will not unwind easily when you pull them apart.

5. When you have a group of adjacent strands in each hand, loop each group over a separate hook (Figure 2-24) and start backing up, allowing the unseparated portion of the thread to dangle freely beneath the V-shaped point of separation. As the two groups are pulled over the hooks, the unseparated portion will begin to spin and untwist. To aid in this spinning, the dangling end of the thread should be clear of the floor. If it does touch the floor, use your left hand to hold both groups of separated strands and your right hand to raise the dangling thread, letting it slip over your palm as you move backward. The higher your hooks are, the sooner the thread will clear the floor. As soon as it does, transfer one group of separated strands back to your right hand so you can keep the groups widely separated as you move back.

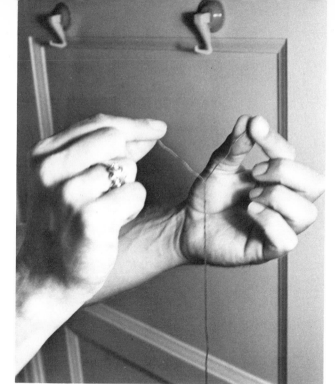

2-23.

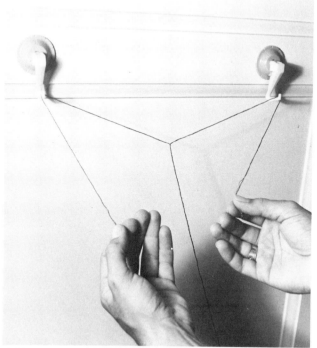

2-24.

6. It is possible to complete the separation of a long piece of thread without a jam-up. However, it is not unusual for a snag to develop at the V-point between the two hooks (Figure 2-25). If this occurs, drop the two already separated units from your hands and move to the V-point. Pick up the two units, one in each hand, near the hooks and apply enough pressure to tighten the V-point into a T-shape. Maintaining tension, transfer the unit from your right hand to your left, but keep the separated units as far apart as possible, allowing them to converge only in your left hand. Reach in and pull on the single six-strand unit of thread below the hooks (Figure 2-26). Then open your right hand to allow the six strands to spin out. This will release the jam-up. You may have to stroke the single six-strand unit from below the snag to its end several times with your right hand to smooth it out. Holding onto the threads as above, continue to back up. Let your right hand open from time to time to allow the bottom strand to spin. If there is another jam-up, repeat the procedure.

2-25.

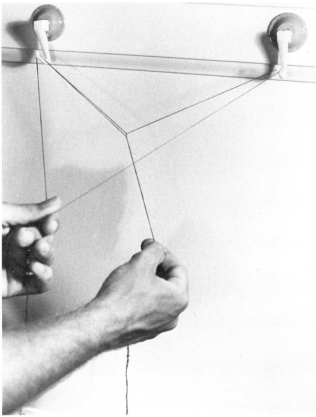

2-26.

7. When the thread has been completely separated, immediately let each of the two lengths fall to the floor. This will keep them from balling up, as they have gone through a considerable amount of intertwining with their separation. With your arms wide apart, lean over and pick up one three-strand length with both hands, lifting it above your head and allowing the two ends to spin until they stop (Figure 2-27). If these two spinning ends get together, forget it! You may as well throw that thread away. It's easier to unscramble an omelet. This is why it is not advisable to work with the entire skein but with shorter pieces.

8. When the length of separated thread has stopped spinning, drape it over a chair or a clothesline strung in your workroom, where it will not be disturbed. Do the same with the second length of separated thread, keeping the two far enough apart so they won't rewind together.

It is also possible to split the six-strand thread into two-strand units. First separate the adjacent strands into one group of two strands and one group of four strands. When these units have been completely separated, divide the four-strand unit in half, using the same procedures as before. To obtain one-strand units, it is best to divide the six strands into three two-strand units, each of which can then be divided in half. A single strand can also be separated from a three-strand unit, but it is almost impossible to extract one strand from the unbroken six-strand unit. Single strands can be wound around an empty spool for safekeeping.

Six-strand embroidery thread comes in a multitude of colors; both American and French manufacturers have outstanding selections. On very rare occasions requiring unusual matches, you may wish to dye your own. I suggest that you start with white thread and use cold-water or batik dyes instead of hot-water dyes, since uniform color is hard to control in the latter.

The same procedures used for determining the amount of rug yarn required for your project can be used for calculating the total number of embroidery skeins you will need. These threads, however, do not have dye-lot numbers. If you want to make a large project, buy a whole box of skeins. A box almost always contains only one dye lot. Arrange when you buy it to return unused skeins; most stores are more than willing to refund money on unbroken skeins. So over-buy!

2-27.

3

Equipment

THE FRAME

Have you ever tried to dance in a hammock? That is just about what punch stitchery would be like without a frame. For the needle to go through the background cloth and for the stitches to hold properly, the cloth must be stretched taut on a frame. You do not want to go chasing after the cloth with the needle. The frame will hold the cloth firmly in place.

You can make or buy a simple, rectangular frame of four wooden strips. It should be equipped with a stand and attached in a way that allows the frame to flip over so that you can work on both sides of the cloth conveniently (Figure 3-1).

There is actually quite a bit of activity on the back side of a frame. Whenever you start a new piece of thread, an inch or two has to be pulled through the eye of the needle at the rear of the cloth before stitching can begin. Until you get the manual dexterity to feel under the cloth for the end of the thread, you will have to flip over the frame to see what you are doing. If you pull the wrong thread, you unravel what you have already done. In addition, when you clip or glue hanging threads, you will definitely have to take a close look at the rear of the cloth. If you accidentally cut a thread in the background cloth, you could ruin your work completely.

3-1.

Your rectangular frame should be, if possible, as wide as your largest project is going to be plus 6 or 8 inches. The extra width allows you to fasten the background cloth to the frame while keeping the design area well away from the wood. For smaller projects, you can reduce the size of your work area without the aid of a hard-to-find stick-shrinker by placing one or two smaller frames on top of the rotating frame (Figure 3-2) and clamping them in place with C-clamps (Figure 3-3). Use prefabricated picture frames, which are available at variety stores and hobby shops in various sizes.

In Figure 3-2, frame 2 is acting as the support for the working frame, frame 3, to which the cloth will be attached. The working frame can also be set into the supporting frame (Figure 3-4). In either case, check to see that the working frame has perfectly squared corners so the cloth can be properly attached (see below). Using more than two additional frames without any inset will create a pyramid and make your working area too high for comfort.

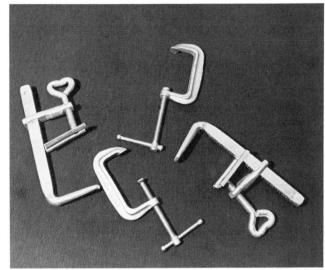

3-3.

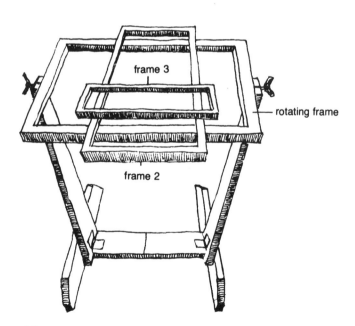

3-2.

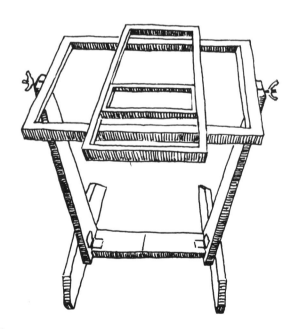

3-4.

With small projects the length of the frame, like the width, should be constructed to allow the design to clear the inside edge of the wood on all four sides when the background cloth is stapled in place. With larger projects a frame can be made that will allow the width to fit within the vertical members of the frame, although the length will often exceed that of the horizontal bars. This means that the work must proceed section by section, with the cloth moved up to a new position on the frame and restapled each time. To cut down on the number of moves you have to make to finish the piece, the horizontal dimensions of the frame should be as wide as possible. The more repositioning you have to do, the greater the chances of cutting the cloth.

The frame should not only be large enough to accommodate your largest project, if possible, but also the height of the stand should be constructed so that you can work comfortably while seated. To determine the proper height, sit in an armless chair with your arms parallel to your body. Raise your forearms to right angles with your upper arms. The distance that your hands are from the floor is the height that the top surface of the frame should be. The upright members of the stand should also be the same height. In calculating the height, be sure to use the chair you will be working in, along with any pillows added for seating comfort. For easy storage, I suggest you get a stand with a folding base (Figure 3-5).

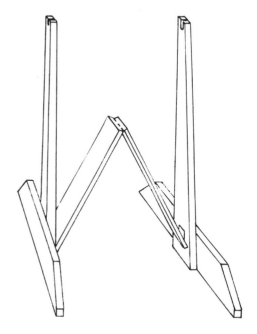

3-5.

OTHER TOOLS AND SUPPLIES

You will have your hands on scissors more often than anything except needles and thread. Your scissors must be both sharp and compliant. They must be cared for as well as respected, because, when you wish to cut a thread, you should cut it and not erode it in two. Never let another person use your scissors; these tools tend to conform to the pressure of the user's hands. It would be like having your car not function well after someone else has driven it.

I recommend that you get a pair of embroidery scissors about 3½ inches in length (Figure 3-6, left). The blades should be at an angle from the finger holes to allow you to cut thread flush with the surface of the material, and they should be perfectly balanced so that yarn can be snipped with the tips alone. Try them out before you buy.

For extremely fine work with embroidery thread of six or less strands, I suggest that you use surgical scissors (also called iris scissors) with evenly sharp points (Figure 3-6, right). It is most important to hold them to the light with the flat sides perpendicular to your eyes to make sure that there are no small Vs where the tips of the blades come to one point. If there are none, the scissors can be used for delicate pushing of threads through cloth, but otherwise, a single filament of a thread can get caught in the Vs and pull out a whole row of punching when the scissors are withdrawn. If you happen to find two perfect pairs, you should buy them. Do not let the jolly old scissors sharpener sharpen them for you, as he will ruin them. Send them to a surgical-supply company; such companies have a service for resharpening the instruments they sell. Resharpening takes some time, which is the reason you should have more than one pair.

Before you attach the cloth to the frame, gather the rest of the supplies and tools you will need. Get a roll of 3-inch gummed tape and cut it into 1-foot lengths. Make two equal folds lengthwise in each strip, which will give you three-ply strips, each 1 foot long and 1 inch wide. The purpose of the tape is to create a solid line of holding surface along the length of the cloth as it is stapled into the wood. Without the three-ply strips, the cloth would be held only at the two spots where each staple goes through the cloth to the wood.

The proper type of staple is also important. It is necessary to use sharply pointed, ceiling-tile staples, because the points must go into the cloth by separating the threads but without shearing them; spade-end staples that have flat entering surfaces will chisel your cloth apart (Figure 3-7). You should have two types of staplers and staples: lightweight, for preliminary tacking, and heavy-duty, for more permanent attaching.

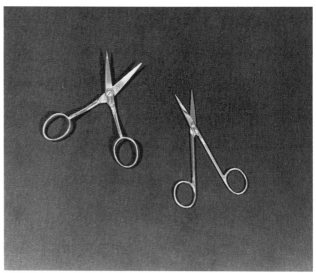

3-6.

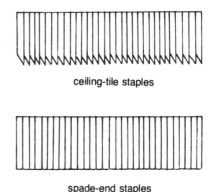

ceiling-tile staples

spade-end staples

3-7.

Some recommended staplers are shown in Figure 3-8. To get the maximum holding power, shoot the staples in at a 45-degree angle instead of perpendicular to it. That way, each staple provides two pressure points on the cloth (Figure 3-9). If you have to remove a staple, use the point of a screwdriver to pry it up (Figure 3-10).

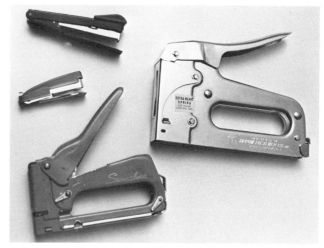

3-8. Some recommended staplers, clockwise from upper left: Bostitch B-8, Arrow T-50, Swingline 101, and Swingline Tot 50.

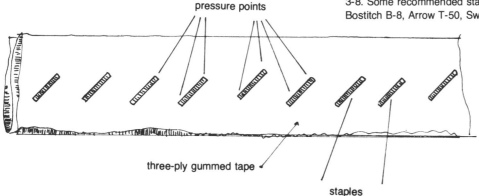

pressure points

three-ply gummed tape

staples

3-9.

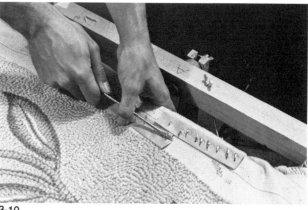

3-10.

ATTACHING CLOTH TO THE FRAME

First of all, remember that for any piece of stitchery, there has to be surplus material outside of the design area in order to staple the cloth to the frame without marring the design. I suggest that, whatever the size of your project, you buy a sufficient overage of material to allow an extra 5 to 6 inches on every side. For a map measuring 3 feet by 2 feet, for instance, figure on 46 inches for one dimension (36 + 5 + 5) and 34 inches for the other dimension (24 + 5 + 5).

As soon as you have cut your rectangle of cloth, use a sewing machine and thread that contrasts with the background sharply for better visibility to stitch at least one line of thread all around the perimeter of the cloth, about 1 inch in from each raw outer edge, to keep the cloth from unraveling. The stitched line should coincide with the warp threads vertically and with the weft threads horizontally, and it should be reinforced with a second line of machine stitching approximately ¼ inch inside the first line of stitching. To ensure that the machine-stitched lines are straight, one of the woven threads in the 1-inch margin along each side of the material can be "pulled," that is, withdrawn, from the cloth. Simply snip the thread at each end of the line to be withdrawn and pull the entire thread out of the material. This will give you an open-looking space that you can stitch along just as you would a line drawn with a ruler.

In addition to the machine stitching, it will be necessary to establish a *thread line* — a reference line that will enable you to get your cloth on the frame with the horizontal threads of the cloth exactly parallel to the horizontal members of the frame (Figure 3-11). The way to unmistakably establish a thread line is to follow one thread of the cloth and baste along it from one side of the cloth to the other with a contrasting-color thread (Figure 3-12). This thread line will be positioned on the outer edge of one horizontal member of the frame.

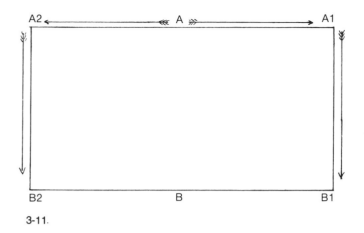

3-11.

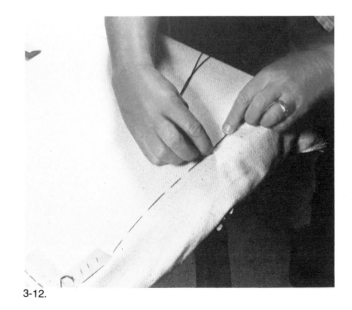

3-12.

40

Once the cloth has been stapled to the frame along this line, you will be able to baste the three additional thread lines, one along each vertical member of the frame and one along the remaining horizontal member of the frame (Figure 3-13). Thereafter, whenever the cloth has to be repositioned in order to work a new section, the vertical thread lines will ensure that the same lateral tension is used, thereby minimizing the risk of distorting the design. If the cloth is so finely woven that the horizontal or vertical thread line cannot be followed, reference lines can be established by measuring and marking your background cloth at constant distances along the edges at 1-inch intervals and basting along the lines from point to point.

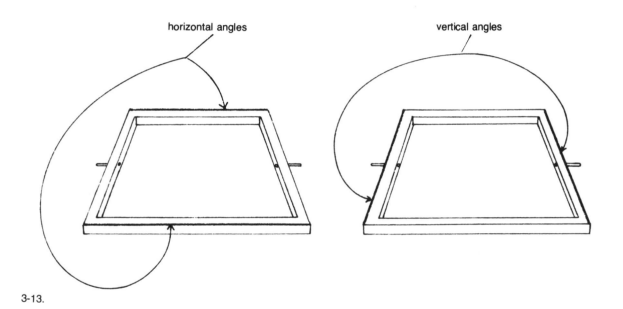

horizontal angles   vertical angles

3-13.

Putting the material on a standing frame is like putting a wheel on an automobile. You can't tighten all the lugs at once, and you can't staple all the sides at once. First you position the cloth; then you draw it tighter by degrees. No big deal.

1. Begin by placing the cloth over the frame, with the basted horizontal thread line on the outer edge of one horizontal bar. Usually you will want to work the design from the top downward, so the thread line will be positioned on the upper bar. If you wish to work from the bottom of the design up to the top, place the thread line on the lower bar. At a point midway from each end of the bar you prefer, tack the cloth in place with five or six lightweight staples spaced out to cover about 4 inches of cloth. For reference, consider this midway point as point A (Figure 3-14; see Figure 3-11 for position of A).

2. Walk around the frame to the second horizontal bar and, at its midway point, opposite point A, grab a handful of cloth close to the frame and pull it tight enough to keep the cloth from sagging between the two points (Figure 3-15). Refer to this second point as B. Place a T-square against the frame to check the verticality of the threads between A and B (Figure 3-16), then place five lightweight staples at B to hold the cloth.

3-14.

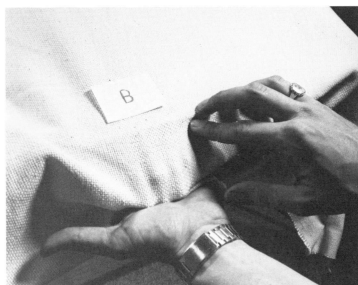
3-15.

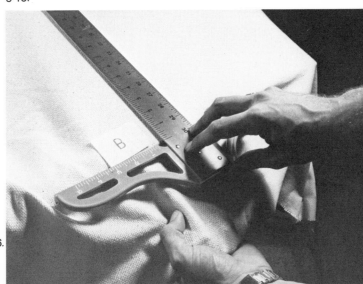
3-16.

3. Return to point A and, making sure the thread line is on the outer edge of the frame, attach the cloth at A with five heavy-duty staples, shooting them through a three-ply strip of gummed tape, which you can place directly over the lightweight staples already there (Figure 3-17). Then move to one end of the same horizontal bar, at the corner of the frame, to attach the cloth at what we will call point A-1. Grab the cloth at this corner to tighten it and, making sure the horizontal thread line is on the outer edge of the bar, shoot five heavy-duty staples through a strip of gummed tape along the horizontal bar. The basted thread line may bow in or out between those two points now, but it will be straightened out later. After you have attached the cloth at one end of the horizontal bar, move to corner A-2 at the opposite end and, again pulling the cloth with maximum pressure from point A to point A-2, attach the cloth with heavy-duty staples through a strip of three-ply paper. Again, make sure that the thread line is on the outer edge of the frame.

4. To give more strength at corners A-1 and A-2, shoot three heavy-duty staples, through gummed paper, along the vertical bar at each corner. The main horizontal thread line is now positioned firmly enough to allow you to baste in the vertical thread lines, starting at each stapled corner and finishing at each unstapled corner (Figure 3-18). After you have completed basting those lines, you can locate and baste in the remaining horizontal thread line along the outer edge of horizontal bar B.

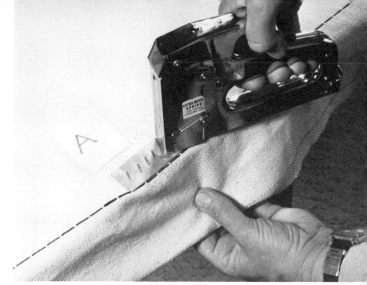

3-17.

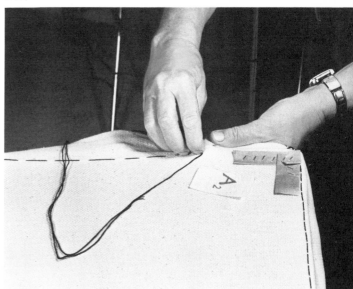

3-18.

5. You now have only to staple the cloth while pulling each basted thread line into position at the outer edge of the frame. You will note that stretching the basted lines at the two remaining corners of the frame (points B-1 and B-2) will take some effort. To aid in setting these corners, which should be done before you heavy-duty staple around the cloth, you can use a cloth-stretching tool, called canvas pliers, which can be purchased at art-supply stores (Figure 3-19, right). (Get the regular,. chrome-plated variety instead of the heavy-duty pliers, because they will not rust.) At each corner, pull the cloth into position with the pliers, staple through a paper strip on the horizontal bar, and then staple through an overlapping paper strip on the vertical bar. When the corners are secure, complete the stapling, using heavy-duty staples and the three-ply paper strips. I suggest that, in your stapling tour around the frame, you check with a T-square from time to time to assure yourself that the threads of the stretched cloth are truly horizontal and vertical.

6. There is one more point to make about attaching the cloth to the frame. After you have completed stitching a section of the design, you must remove the staples and reposition the cloth for the next section. Now, when the cloth is filled with stitches, as it would be for a rug, and you have to shift to the next section, you will have to penetrate punched yarn with the staples, at least along one horizontal bar. You may find that even ½-inch staples just won't hold. In that case, I suggest that you use 1½-inch flat-headed nails, hammering each one through a small square of three-ply paper (Figure 3-20). The best way to extract these nails is with needle-nose pliers (Figure 3-19, left).

If you are working on a small project, instead of stretching the cloth over the entire standing frame, you will naturally staple the cloth to a small frame, which you will clamp to the large frame. To hold the small frame in position for stapling, the best tool is a wood vise. The place to find one, if you do not have your own, is a do-it-yourself frame shop. Be sure to protect the cloth and frame from picking up dirt by placing paper against the jaws of the vise. Remember that the dimensions of the frame should be slightly larger than those of the intended design.

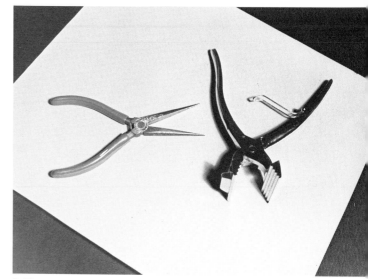

3-19.

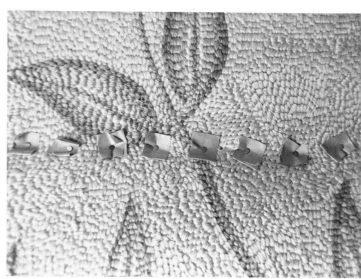

3-20.

LIGHT SOURCES FOR STITCHING

In stitching large designs, the tungsten light from a regular bulb is adequate. If you are right-handed, the light source should be over your left shoulder; conversely, if you are left-handed, it should be over your right shoulder. For stitching highly detailed designs, a magnifying light is useful.

You can buy, for a rather heavy sum, a swiveling lamp equipped with a magnifying glass and three small, fluorescent light tubes. I have one called a Dazor Floating Fixture (Model M-209), which can be clamped to the frame or to a nearby table (Figure 3-21). It is possible to get the same lamp with a weighted base. *I must warn those among you with complex eyeglasses or eye deficiencies to be sure to check with your eye specialist whether or not you can use this type of light magnification.*

Fluorescent lighting will absolutely deaden the color reflected by your yarn or thread. Choose your colors under daylight or regular electric light and don't lose heart by what you see under fluorescent light. You may ask, "Why use fluorescent light?" The answer is that it casts no shadows. You will be involved enough without working in your own shadow.

Fluorescent lighting doesn't heat up the way tungsten lighting does, but it is the world's worst fader of colors. A fluorescent-light fixture should always be turned off when you are not using it to stitch. While tungsten light will not fade colors, if it is allowed to get too close to linen cloth, its heat will take the tension out of the linen and make it brittle.

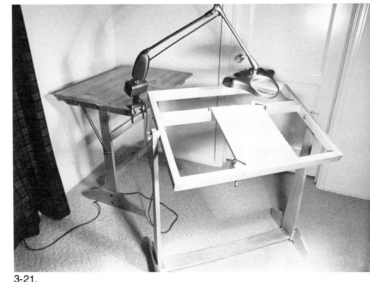

3-21.

4

Design

In stitchery, as in politics, ad-libbing can get messy. To execute your project properly, you need a definite design — a picture or decorative pattern of some sort — and a method of transferring the image to the cloth as a guide for the actual stitching.

CHOOSING THE DESIGN

The inspiration for your design can come from anywhere. With me, I guess it all began whèn I saw Douglas Fairbanks as Robin Hood. He was always squashing whole bunches of Black Prince John's men and swinging on the ever-present ropes dangling around the castle. Real neat-o! And he was something else climbing up those drawbridges, jumping all over Sherwood Forest, shooting arrows, and all — except when things got going good, he had to stop and save that silly old Maid Marian — who was always running away from something bad, although I never could figure out what. Not then. Gee whiz, did I have Sherwood fever?

But in time I became a witty high-school sophomore and outgrew all that Saxon junk, until one day I read *Ivanhoe,* and the medieval fever got me again.

Then I went off to college, where we lived for the Saturday game, and I began to notice (which took up all my time) that the girls had tighter-fitting skin. In my junior year I read *The Idylls of the King* and was really bitten by the feudal bug. But I recovered all right and graduated, *summa cum lucky,* and went out into the world, where I became very involved. I learned to distinguish brands of Scotch and go on no sleep, and I dated bunches of knowing and ever-so-lovely young ladies. As things go, I got married, and my very beautiful wife had for us a couple of yowlers, whom I despaired of ever reaching puberty — let alone college. Oh, occasionally, I noticed something about the Middle Ages — but I was kept so *busy!*

Then, when my offspring, as they usually do, up and got married, my wife and I had time to become very traveled — we dug Mayan ruins in Yucatan; we searched Cuzco and Ephesus, Sikri Fatareh and Machu Picchu, Kutb-Minar and Sacsahuaman. One day, on the way to somewhere — for the life of me I can't remember where — we dropped into Vienna's Hofburg Museum and saw the Charlemagne Room. And there in front of me, in all their total wonder, were those fantastically stitched heraldic tunics, copes, and vestments, the likes of which have never been equaled.

After all of my wandering to see the wonders of the ancient worlds, I had come home. The feudal bug had laid me low. I realized then that, with all the derring-do, it was the heraldic arts of the Middle Ages that had all along stirred my imagination since childhood. And that's why I started stitching and drawing upon the sun-bright heraldry of the Dark Ages for my designs.

Anything you see can spark an inspiration for your designs — a mental picture, a color photo, an ornament, a painting, and so forth. (With all the "so forths" lying around, you should surely find one to fit your order.) Whether your design is an original sketch or a commercial illustration, you should obtain several photostatic or xerographic copies of it in black and white so you can experiment with colors and work out the details without ruining the original.

Color is a complicated business, which I will discuss in the next chapter. May I caution you that while you can have some jolly times filling in the black-and-white copies of your design with colored chalk or paints — remember that you cannot always find the yarns or threads to match these colors. You may be wasting time; you may have to compromise. Once upon a time I drew a beautiful, pastel, Japanesy tree in watercolors, which pleased me no end (Figure C-8). And with much, much labor I transferred the tree to a great big piece of paper — 6½ by 7½ feet in size to be exact — and colored it all in with lovely pastel chalk. It was to be a john rug fit for a princess. Then I went to the big store in the city to buy yarns matching the beautiful colors of the drawing I had wrought, and lo! there were none. Nobody made colors like my pretty tree. I was up the creek without a paddle. Throwing caution to the winds, I made the tree rug anyhow (Figure C-9), but, as you can see, it wasn't what I had in mind.

To avoid unforeseen changes in plan, go to several stores first and see if anybody makes colors like you have in mind. If they do and if you can get enough yarn of the same dye lot of each color to fill your design, buy your yarn. Only then do you match up chalk with the colors of the yarn and fill in your large design. If the colors you had in mind are not available, you will have to change some ideas, but your basic concept can remain intact. At least you won't have to ad-lib color placement on the spur of the moment, and you can proceed to a very satisfactory piece of art without blowing a blood-pressure gasket. You have to live with what is available. That is, unless you want to dye your own yarn. But before you start boiling vats of dye in your kitchen, you had better check the price of a small but virulent divorce!

ENLARGING THE DESIGN

Once you have refined your design to its final version, you are ready to transfer it to the cloth. However, if you want your project to be larger than the design you made, you must first enlarge your completed drawing by using a system of small and large grids.

1. The first step is to transfer the design to graph paper, which is already ruled with a set number of square boxes per inch (usually five or ten). You make this transfer by inserting a sheet of carbon paper between the design and the graph paper and tracing over the design with a very hard pencil.

If your original design has been executed on heavy paper, such as that used for photostatic copies, you may find it difficult to apply proper pencil pressure to transfer it to the graph paper. In that case, you can trace the completed design onto a sheet of technical-grade tracing paper, which can then be placed over the carbon and transferred to the graph papers. Secure both tracing paper and design together with masking tape and hold both sheets against a strong light source, such as a window or a light box. Trace the design with a soft-lead pencil. After you have completed the tracing, spray it with a fixative or clear acrylic coating to protect it and decrease smearing. In tracing, always turn the work so that you can make backhand strokes, using wrist action as opposed to finger action — each stroke is smoother that way. Also, try to keep your hand in a position that will not smudge what you have already traced.

In tracing your final design onto graph paper, make sure the vertical and horizontal elements of the design coincide with the vertical and horizontal lines of the graph paper. Use a T-square to ensure alignment if necessary. The small boxes of the graph paper are usually sectioned off into larger square units by heavier lines; starting at one corner of the design, number these squares consecutively, first in a horizontal direction across the bottom or top of the design and then in a vertical direction along one side of the design. These numbered lines will be used for reference in enlarging the work, so if the graph paper is not printed with heavy lines, mark off the larger units of 1-inch squares yourself with a pencil and T-square (Figure 4-1). It is also possible for you to draw a grid directly on your tracing instead of transferring it to graph paper. But you've got to be right the first time.

2. You are now going to enlarge the design by drawing a corresponding grid of squares on a large sheet of white wrapping paper. First decide what size you would like your finished work to be. Suppose you choose a height of 24 inches. Measure the height of your original design and divide the 24 inches by the smaller number (let's say it is 6 inches) to determine the scale of the enlargement. In this case, the enlargement is four times the original size (24 divided by 6). This means that all the original measurements must be multiplied by four to obtain the correct proportions in the larger version. If the original design is 4 inches wide, the width of the enlarged design must be 16 inches.

4-1.

3. To draw the new grid, tape your large sheet of paper to a drawing board or any other right-angled object with a flat surface and use a T-square to draw a rectangle the size of your intended project. (If your design is in the shape of a circle or a trapezoid or anything except a square or rectangle, your cloth will still have to be rectangular so that you can pull equal tension to work your design. You cannot attach a circle to a frame and maintain tension. Hypertension — yes!) Mark off the top line and one vertical line with dots indicating the distance between each numbered unit.

(If the units are to be 4 square inches, for example, mark off every 4 inches along both lines.) Then use a T-square to draw vertical and horizontal lines through each dot. If the design is complicated and you need additional reference points within the 4-inch squares, measure the distance between the smaller boxes of your original graph-paper grid, multiply that figure by your enlargement factor (here, four), and mark off these additional units horizontally and vertically on your large grid. Number the large grid in the same manner as you numbered the original smaller one, and you are ready to enlarge your design.

4. To transfer the enlarged design, determine where each line of the original crosses a line in the smaller grid and plot these coordinate points on the corresponding lines of the larger grid, marking them off with small dots. Use the numbered squares on each grid as a guide in locating the dots. By connecting the dots on the large grid, like you used to do in the Sunday funnies, you can construct the enlarged version of the design accurately and simply (Figure 4-2).

I suggest that you transfer the enlarged design to another sheet of paper, either by tracing over it on technical-grade tracing paper or by using a piece of carbon paper. The work of transferring the design onto cloth tends to destroy it, and you should have more than one good copy of your enlarged design. To make sure the pencil or carbon lines won't smear, go over the design carefully with a sharp-pointed felt-tipped pen.

Use white laundry paper for your full-scale drawing. This is the paper that laundries use to wrap up piles of shirts (if you're lucky enough to have a pile), sheets, and other bulky packages. Unfortunately, clear plastic is appearing on the market for this purpose. The hand laundries still wrap in this heavy-rag-content paper, and if you find a source, buy a partial roll. It isn't cheap, but it won't spoil. This paper will accept felt-pen marking, tempera paints, pastel chalks, perforations made while tracing, and many, many foldings and unfoldings without tearing. For larger projects, long strips of this paper can be taped together, preferably with ½-inch or 1-inch Magic Transparent Scotch Tape No. 810. It will not brown or turn brittle, and it is very pliable.

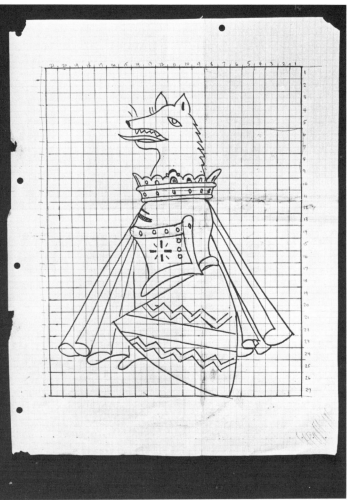

4-2.

50

TRANSFERRING THE DESIGN TO THE CLOTH

PRETESTING THE CLOTH

A small bit of the cloth you plan to use for your project should be tested to see if it will accept the transfer of the design. It is silly to subject a large piece of expensive material to the caprices of experimentation. To test which degree of sponginess will best receive the carbon transfer, place six to eight layers of newspaper under one portion of the test cloth, which should be taped onto a board as tautly as possible and fastened with masking tape to prevent wrinkles (Figure 4-3). Another portion of the same cloth can be placed on the bare board to see if this degree of hardness is better for design-transfer clarity. Different fixing sprays can also be tested at this time to see what effect they have on the cloth. I found Blair's No Odor Spray Fix most suitable.

CENTERING THE DESIGN

This section illustrates how to center a design on a cloth against a glass background, the technique that is used for a small design with more than rug-sized intricacy of detail.

1. Using the thread lines already established on the cloth (see Chapter 2) to keep the warp threads perpendicular and the weft threads horizontal, the cloth (linen in this instance) is secured on the back of the base (Figure 4-4).

4-4.

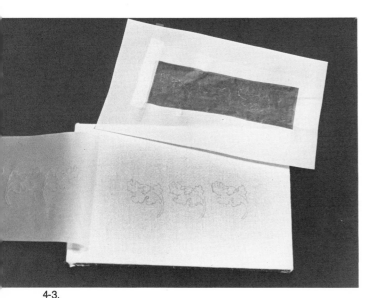

4-3.

2. As the drawing board is to be the control edge for the T-square, the linen-covered glass is lightly attached to the drawing board with tape (Figure 4-5).

3. The horizontal and vertical threads are aligned in square formation in relation to the drawing board (Figure 4-6).

4. The design is placed on the cloth (Figure 4-7).

5. The design is centered and squared in relation to the center of the cloth (Figure 4-8).

6. The design is taped to the cloth and covered with a proper-sized piece of carbon paper (Figure 4-9).

7. The carbon is cut large enough to cover the design (Figure 4-10).

8. The carbon is taped to the cloth (Figure 4-11).

9. The design is ready for tracing (Figure 4-12).

10. To make sure that no carbon will be smudged on the cloth, a cover should be placed over the part of the work outside of the design area and over the entire project when you are not working (Figure 4-13).

While you are centering your design on the cloth, it can be located on the working frame at the same time. This helps to reduce handling of the work. The more a piece is handled, the more chance there is to louse it up. Figure 4-14 shows a design being aligned with the frame. It is checked to see that there is comfortable working room inside the wood-bounded area.

4-6.

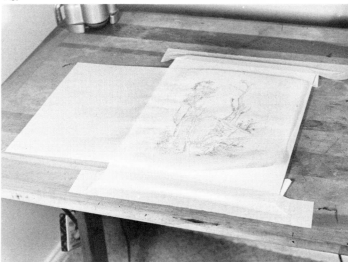

4-7.

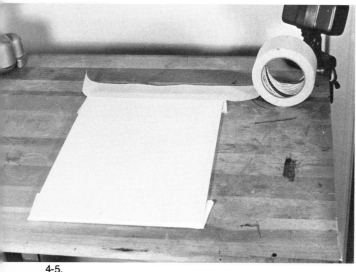

4-5.

4-8.

4-9.

4-12.

4-10.

4-13.

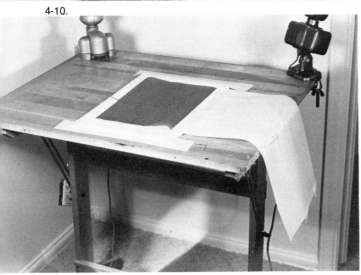

4-11.

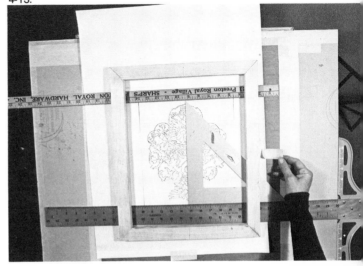

4-14.

WHAT TO TRACE

Only the general outlines of a design should be transferred onto the cloth. Minor details will not transfer clearly enough to be of any use. Even minute variances of tension applied to the cloth on the frame will tend to distort and scramble fine detail and will just leave a mess of lines on the cloth, which will make hitting the holes between the warp and weft threads very difficult. In the Tree Rug, for example, only the outlines of the leaves were transferred, even though the internal design of each leaf was different. By using a protractor with two steel points, also called a *bow* (Figure 4-15), fine details can be spotted on the cloth without making any pencil marks. As soon as a spot is located on the background cloth, a pin can be inserted to mark the place where the thread is to enter.

The design must also be adapted to the project you have in mind. For example, if you are using a tree design for a looped rug, which tends to flatten with use, avoid sharp angles. The branches should come out of the trunk as close to perpendicular as possible. Acute angles fill up with stitches and, in a small area with different colors, give a smeary, bulky appearance. In Figure 4-16, which shows the trunks of an elm and an oak tree, you will see that the loops delineating the elm trunk will be a living mess, while those of the oak trunk, since they have wide-open branch angles, will be clear.

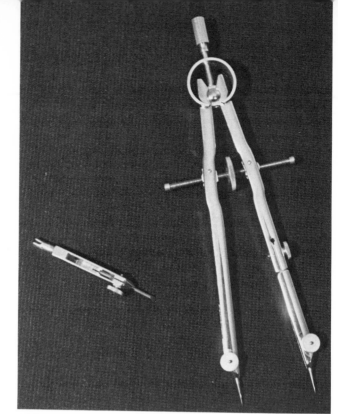

4-15.

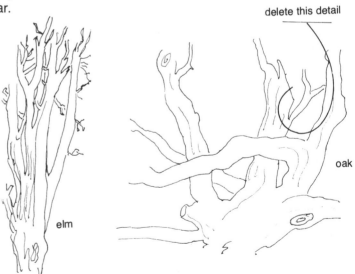

delete this detail

elm

oak

4-16.

TRACING THE DESIGN

First, determine which side of the work is going to be displayed. If you are making a map hanging of the United States, for example, the surface of the cloth next to the carbon paper will be the face of the finished work, and California will be on the left. But if you are making a punch rug of the United States, you are going to be walking on the surface away from the carbon paper, and the design will have to be traced from the reverse side, that is, with California on the right side so that it will be out West again when you flip your work over. Tracing the design onto the cloth can be done in three ways:

1. For small designs with many curves and much detail, such as the Illeshazy Arms and the Mexico Map (Figures C-3 and C-4), arrange the cloth on a hard tracing surface like glass or a drawing board. Use a hard pencil with a slightly rounded point so it doesn't cut the design paper. Make the tracing in short strokes with wrist movements. In tracing onto linen or any other cloth, rotate the board so that your hand always works at the lower border of the design and use outward, backhand strokes where possible. Except for the pencil, do not exert much pressure on the design itself, since the carbon will rub off on the linen. Wherever possible, the pencil should not be picked up between strokes, because you will tend to retrace in these areas, which will give you a smeary line on the cloth. Never retrace a line if you are not sure that you have traced it or if you think you might have missed it. A double-traced line on the cloth is confusing and may extend into a section of the cloth which will not be covered by thread. You can tell where you have traced by sighting the design against the light. The pencil marks will leave a shiny line, which is why a pencil and not a stylus should be used. When you think you have traced all of the lines, leave the design attached to the cloth on one side by masking tape and carefully lift the design and the carbon from the paper. If there are any gaps, carefully lower the paper again and trace the gaps. *Be sure* that you only trace in the gaps; *do not* retrace. Check the design as many times as you want, but don't retrace.

2. For designs with few details, such as the Clopton Arms or the more generalized maps of England and Europe, and on cloth that is bumpy — not finely woven — the design is transferred by punching the pattern with a very sharp-pointed, very hard-leaded pencil in a series of dots through the design lines. (The pencil should not have a needle point, as the lead will break, the pencil will jump, and you will scar the cloth.) These dots can be as close together as $1/8$ inch. The dots should perforate the design and invade the linen or cloth. If the design is backed by a mattress board, as the England and Europe maps (Figures C-7 and C-5) were, the point of the pencil will go through the cloth into the mattress board. The further the pencil point goes into the mattress board, the bigger the dots will be on the cloth.

3. For large, sweeping designs, such as the Tree Rug and the Bird Rug, transfer the design with a pattern-tracing wheel. This procedure will be explained in Chapter 8.

5

Color

We live in a vibratory world. Sound is vibration. Light is vibration. Since light can be broken up into monochromatic or primary colors (those which can't be separated into more than one hue), light *is* color.

Color vibrations are sometimes called *waves,* and our eyes, depending on the amount of eye shadow stuccoed on, perceive 36,000 to 61,000 vibrations per inch.

You have seen a spectrum somewhere — in a kindergarten experiment, a physics lab, or a rainbow. A spectrum is the result of breaking up white light into a band of different-colored lights. This is done by refracting light through a prism. It can also be done by cracking your head. You see the same beautiful colors, but this time they are accompanied by bells, chimes, and cymbals (more vibrations!). This is more painful than the prism method.

From red with 36,000 vibrations per inch through orange, yellow, green, blue, and indigo to violet with 61,000 vibrations per inch, as these vibrations hit the retina and pass through the optic nerve to the brain, you "see" color. When you see a red flag, apart from its political connotations, it means that white light is falling on the flag and all of the other colors of the spectrum are being absorbed by the flag except red, which bounces back with just its number of vibrations per inch and jangles your optic nerve through your eyes at such a frequency that your brain perceives the flag as red. In the case of green, every color is soaked up except green, etc.

STANDARD COLOR TERMINOLOGY

Hue is the name given to a color, such as red, red-orange, purplish-red, ad infinitum.

Value is the darkness or the lightness of a hue, such as a dark red or a light red. A dark hue, or *shade,* has some black added to it, and a light hue, or *tint,* is diluted with white.

Intensity relates to the strength of a color. A color's intensity can be lessened by adding gray to it with various dyes. This doesn't change the hue or value; it just cuts down on its oscillation. *Oscillating colors* seem to have heat waves running across them. They are pure hues, without any gray, so they can liven up a broad area of less intense color (the drops of blood on the breasts of the black eagles in the Illeshazy Arms in Figure C-3, for example). They cannot be used in large areas, because they will give the other colored areas a dead, dark appearance. Your theory of what makes colors seem to vibrate is as good as that of the guy who lives down the street. If you think you have never seen vibrating or oscillating colors and would like to do so, drink about a pint of 100-proof bourbon in half an hour in some dark saloon, then step outside into bright sunlight. If everything you see isn't vibrating, you needn't concern yourself about oscillating colors. Worry about an undertaker — you're dead!

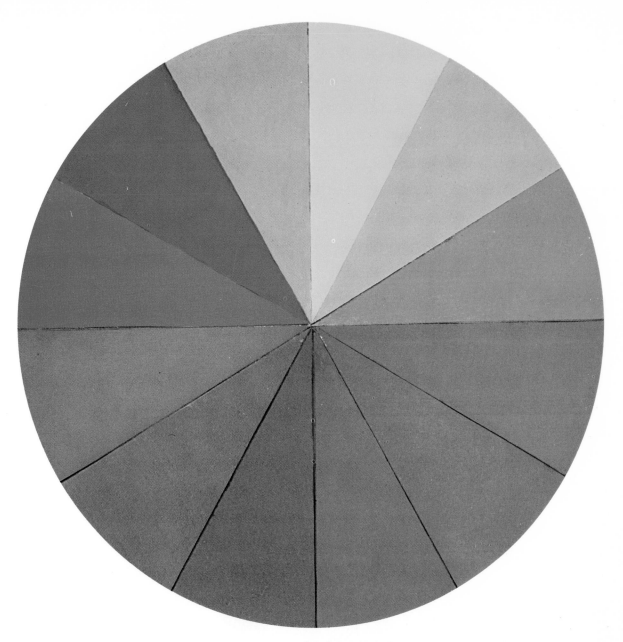

C-1. Color wheel. (From *Weaving and Needlecraft Color Course* by William and Doris Justema, Van Nostrand Reinhold, New York, 1971)

→
C-2. Arms of Clopton, Sussex. (Photograph by Peter Brady)

→
C-3. Arms of Illeshazy, Hungary. (Photograph by John Messina)

Clopton

R.E. ILLES '70

Illésházy

C-4. Map of Mexico. (Photograph by John Messina)

Colors are characterized as either *warm* or *cool*. Warm colors are red (notice how hot you feel when you blush?), orange, and yellow. Cool colors are associated with blue (blue norther, blue ice, shadows on snow, blue with cold). Distance is blue or purple, so blue, blue-green, and blue-violet recede. They are known as *retreating* colors. The reds, oranges, and yellows are called *advancing* colors. Yellow is the weakest of these; it only advances when it is used in contrast with black or other dark hues. Distance will mellow the effect of the so-called advancing colors; at a distance faraway mountains appear gray, but as you approach them, their colors become more and more intense.

C-5. Map of Europe. (Photograph by John Messina)

C-6. Detail of C-5 showing Austria and its borders.

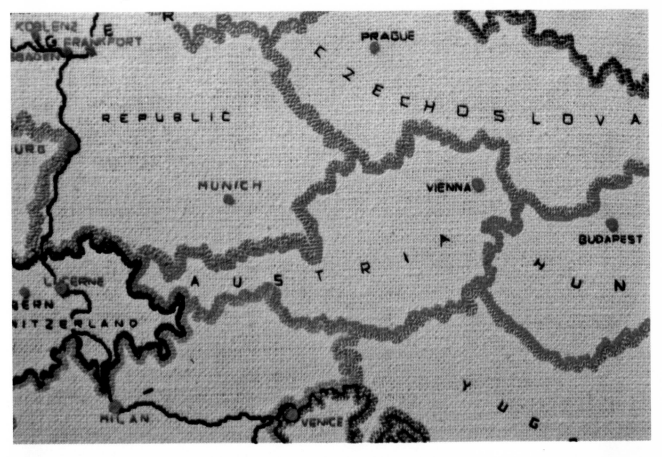

A *color wheel* is a circle cut into twelve or eighteen equal pie-shaped segments of different colors that are displayed in a widening band towards its outer edge (Figure C-1). Although a color wheel will not arbitrate all of your color-selection problems, it will help you to understand that some order does exist.

On a properly prepared color wheel, the hues opposite each other are *complementary*, which means completed or fulfilled. A pair of these colors, when mixed in the proper proportions, yields a neutral, gray color. I don't know whether looking gray is being fulfilled or not — it's being old. Maybe you're supposed to be fulfilled when you're old.

C-8. Original watercolor for the Tree Rug.

C-9. Tree Rug. (Photograph by John Messina)

63

Complementary colors occur naturally in our visual apparatus in *afterimages*. To see what an afterimage is, try the following experiment. Look at a well-lit light bulb for a few seconds. What you see is an intense white light. Now shut your eyes. The filaments now appear black. These black filaments are the afterimage of the white filaments. If you look at a red square for about ten seconds in a strong light, the afterimage will be greenish. If you look at an orange square, then shut your eyes, you will see a blue square. The afterimage of a color is always its complementary. This effect is due to a very complex physiological and psychological procedure. When you look at a red square, for example, the vibrations hitting your retina (the back inside wall of your eye) tire the color-vibration receivers for red. When you shut your eyes, the green you "see" comes from remaining cells that haven't been fatigued by the red-light vibrations.

COLOR RELATIONSHIPS

M. E. Chevreul (1786–1889), renowned chemist and director of the Gobelins tapestry works, set out in his historic *Principles of Harmony and Contrast in Color* several of the laws of color upon which dye technology is still based today. One of his most important and fundamental laws, which will affect your work all of the time, is that colors are modified in appearance by their proximity to other colors, or however he said it in French. This is called the law of *simultaneous contrast*. To demonstrate this law, I suggest that you lay a piece of red yarn and a piece of blue yarn side by side. Your eye will no longer see the red as red and the blue as blue, because each color is modified by its adjacent color. The red will appear orange-red, because orange is the complementary of blue. The blue will appear green-blue, because green is the complementary of red. In general, if two colors are placed together, each appears tinged by the complementary of the other.

It is possible to attain, following this law, a gradation of tints and shades. For instance, suppose you have three values of gold threads, dark, medium, and light. If these colors tend to give a striped effect instead of a smooth modulation from dark to light, you can arrange the threads in the following sequence: dark, dark, dark, medium, medium, medium, medium, light, light, light. Each thread throws a reflection of its color onto the next thread, creating a smooth, graded effect.

Bearing in mind that there are three primary colors, red, blue, and yellow, Chevreul tells us that the secondary color obtained by mixing any two of the primary colors results in the complementary of the remaining third primary color. For example, red and blue mixed together produce purple, which is the complementary of the remaining primary, yellow. Again, he says that black will accentuate any of the lighter colors (or advancing colors) and in doing so make the black seem blacker. And the same holds true in reverse: light colors will accentuate dark colors. This principle is demonstrated by the black border around the bird in the Bird Rug (Figure C-10), the black around the wolf's head in the Clopton Arms (Figure C-2), and the red blood drop in the center of the two black eagles in the Illeshazy Arms (Figure C-3). All of these effects were used to break monotony and accentuate weaker colors.

Near complements may have more verve and spirit than exact complements. To contrast with blue, complement variations, such as yellow-orange or red-orange, may be even livelier or more desirable than pure orange.

Analogous colors are colors that are side by side on the color wheel, such as red, red-orange, and orange. Another group would be yellow, yellow-green, and green. All of the colors on the wheel are analogous to the two colors they are adjacent to. If you use more than four consecutive colors, however, you start to impose on the complementary colors of the first four (see Figure C-1). This tends to make everything complementary to everything else, so your attention will start going around in circles, and you will end up with a mess. There has to be a dominant color scheme. The easiest route to harmony is to limit yourself to a short analogous span. That is, unless you are Mexican — then anything goes!

Another of Chevreul's laws is that when complementary colors are used next to each other, each color appears brighter than by itself. A case in point is the intensity of the small amount of red and green in the Illeshazy cloak (Figure C-3). Red throws its complementary, green, into the green, and green throws its complementary, red, into red, so each color is intensified.

6
Working the Design

PUNCH STITCHING

Most of this book has been about how to get ready to punch something. Now, to punch something at last!

    1. For rugs and heavy clothwork, load the rug needle, as explained in Chapter 2, stick it through the cloth, pull the yarn so that it hangs loose from the point of the needle, and pull the needle out. On every first stitch of a series, hold the hanging piece of yarn until the needle has entered the cloth the second time. This locks the yarn into the cloth; otherwise it might flip right out of the hole like wet spaghetti. Move the needle along the top of the cloth (about ⅜ inch if you want a tightly packed rug; ½ inch if you want it looser) and just punch again and again and again until you get punchy — or have filled up your cloth (Figure 6-1). The only thing you have to remember is to keep the point of the needle close to the material when you move from one punch to the next. If you happen to hit a thread instead of a hole, don't worry; just jab it on through. You can't hurt this cloth!

    2. For linen-backed projects, load the hypo needle, as explained in Chapter 2, stick it through with the thread hanging loose under the cloth, holding the tag end of the thread during the insertion of the second stitch, as stated above, and go at it! With this more delicate fabric, the distance between punches should be shorter, and instead of jabbing when you hit a thread, push with a firm but gentle pressure to get the needle through. Try to keep to the holes as much as possible. That's all there is to it. After a while you'll get your own personal rhythm and away you'll go!

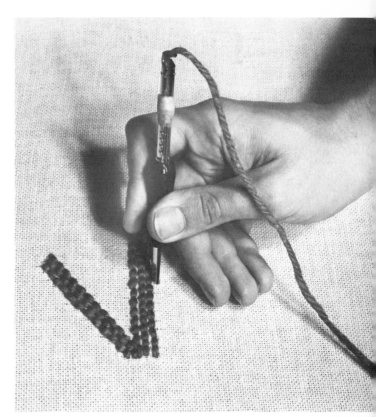

6-1.

For any project, the cycle of a stitch, starting with a loaded needle in your hand, is as follows:

1. Place your finger over the top of the needle to arrest the flow of thread (Figure 6-2).

2. Insert the needle into a hole in the cloth (Figure 6-3).

3. Reach under the cloth and get hold of the thread (Figure 6-4).

4. Withdraw the needle (Figure 6-5).

5. With the point of the needle barely above the cloth, move it to the next hole and slant it at a 45-degree angle in relation to the warp and weft threads of the cloth, or on the bias (Figure 6-6).

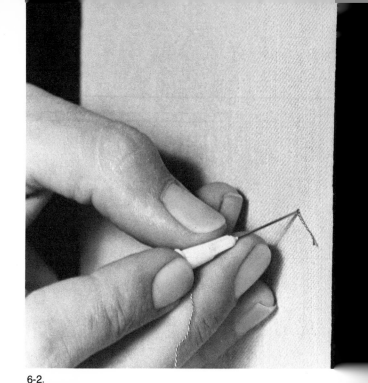

6-2.

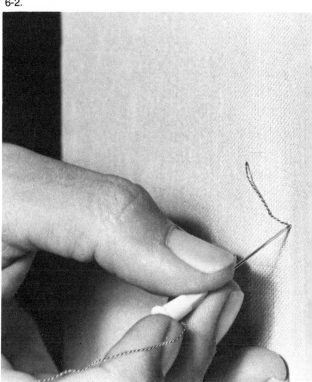

6-3.

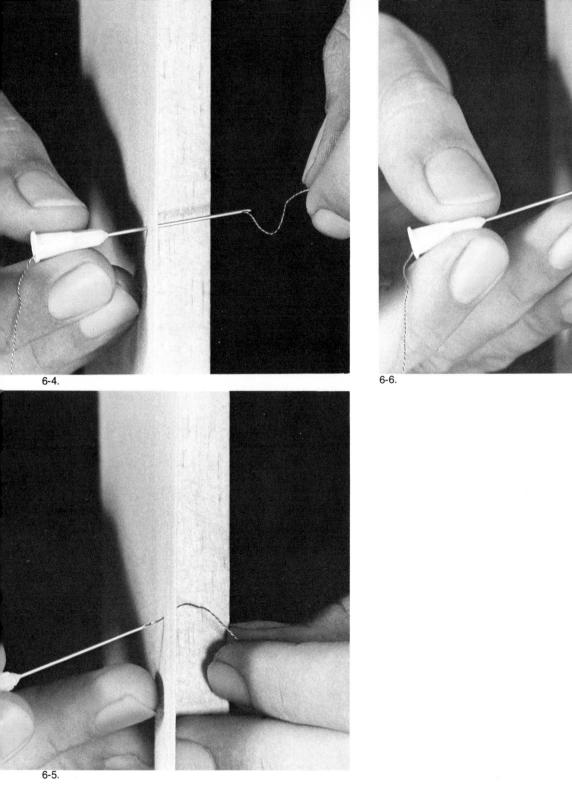

6-4.

6-5.

6-6.

6. Remove your finger from the top of the needle and insert it in the next hole (Figure 6-7).

7. Withdraw the needle for the next stitch, leaving a loop on the back of the cloth (Figure 6-8).

At the end of a cycle of stitches, if you wish to cut the thread or change color, clip the thread that lies along the side of the needle while it is under the cloth. Otherwise you will strip out what you have just put in.

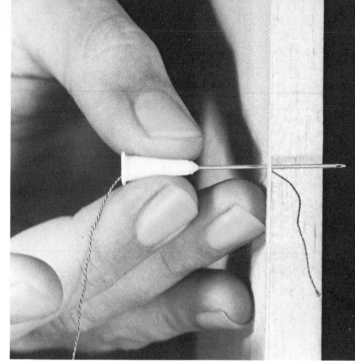

6-7.

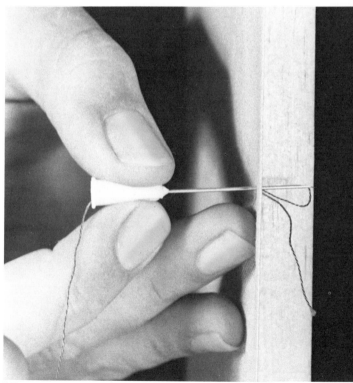

6-8.

To speed up the clipping process and the insertion of the scissors point between the thread and the needle, press with your finger on the point of the needle, pinch the needle between thumb and forefinger, and push. If the thread is tightly packed, the pressure of the needle will prick your finger, so use the side of the scissors to push the needle back. These maneuvers will create a readily visible loop, thereby facilitating snipping and keeping you from cutting into the needle with your precious scissors (Figure 6-9).

If there is any pull whatsoever on the thread that keeps it from slipping through the needle, you will not be depositing thread in the cloth. If there are any short loops *above* the working surface, even though they may be an inch or two away, pull out the thread to one or two stitches beyond that loop and start over. That loop indicates that the stitch was not grabbed, which, in the case of a rug, will snag the work and pull out a length of stitches and, in the case of embroidery, will destroy a tight, smooth surface.

You will often want to control the length of the loops, especially if you intend to display the looped surface of the work and with the price of thread increasing daily. (Do the Arabs control threads, too?) You can keep the depth of stitches uniform with a lawnmower-throttle cable stop tightened onto the hypodermic needle at the required interval (Figure 6-10).

You will find that, in the long run, it is a peachy-keen idea to have several needles for this or any kind of work, one for each color that you are using within a small area. Nothing is more tedious than stopping to pull out one color and insert another into one lone, lorn needle.

6-9.

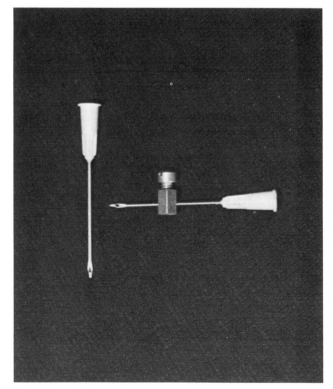

6-10.

PUTTING IN THE BACKGROUND TEXTURE OF A LOOPED DESIGN

The odd assortment of lines that you see in the rug design in Figures 6-11 and 6-12 are not drawn in for the lack of something to do. These lines perform a service in reminding the stitcher not to punch the background in long, straight or slightly curved lines but to vary groups of lines directionally. When the loops in a background are punched in long, straight lines, the loops on the reverse side of the piece (in the case of a rug, the walk-on side) take on a streaked, machined look. By curving and radically changing the direction of groups of punches, you are varying the angles at which the loops on the walk-on side are presented to the light source. The reflecting light results in a uniform, unstreaked area of color. Although this technique is most applicable for rugs, as they tend to have more background area and are viewed from above (where the downward light source makes streaking more apparent), it should also be used for any large, single-colored area.

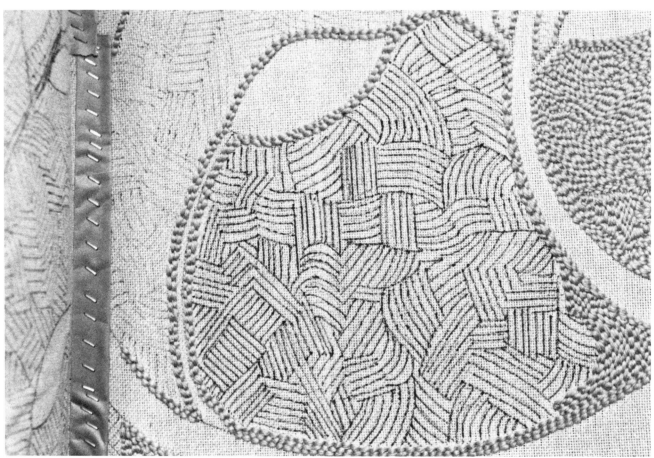

6-11.

OUTLINING THE DESIGN

The outside edge of an object or solid form is the departing point, beyond which you look into space. (If the outside edge happens to be crammed full of blonde, it is unlikely you will look into space.)

In pictures and in cartooning, an outline is represented by a line; in painting, this line is formed by the foreground figure in relation to its background. In stitchery, this departing point into space can be the line between two different colors or a single line of yarn or thread.

6-12.

SEPARATION OF COLORS WITHIN A DESIGN

If two colors of almost the same tonal intensity are next to each other, such as the yellow in the bird's tail in the Bird Rug (Figure C-10) in relation to the golden background or the silver in the mantle of the Illeshazy Arms (Figure C-3) in relation to the neutral background cloth, a definite outline in an intense color or black should be used to separate them.

In inserting a line of punches to form a design outline, loops are often punched inside adjacent loops. If the loops are on the observed surface, as with rugs, they will have to be separated, as loops within loops will dissipate the continuity of the design. This is done simply by pulling the loops apart so that they stand alone. Areas where one color abuts another should be inspected and the interlocking loops separated by using the scissors point to withdraw the invader while you pinch the other with your pinkies. You should start your stitching, if possible, on the inside of a design element and work outward, since it is difficult to separate loops in a tightly packed area. The tight packing itself will cause one loop to get inside the one next to it.

If you are using one thin line of color, especially in a rug, put it in last to ensure that it won't be submerged in a mass of punches. If you put that important bit of color into blank cloth, there is a lower tension on the needle as it comes back through the cloth, and the needle tends to drag a bit of the deposited thread out with it, leaving it short. As subsequent rows of stitches are packed into the cloth, they do not come back out of the hole and therefore have longer loops, which will cover up the first loops put into the blank cloth. To ensure that a thin row of color is definitely apparent in a mass of stitches, punch two rows very close together. This sequence of depositing colors is even more important if you are using wool yarn, because wool is much more compressible than cotton or rayon and the needle will drag it back out of the hole further, especially on blank cloth. An additional insurance in depositing a line of wool in a cotton or rayon cloth is to turn the needle so that the bevel of the point is not facing forward but at a 45-degree angle in relation to the direction to be punched, that is, partially to the side.

OUTLINING INTRICATE DESIGNS

In the case of most maps, coats of arms, and other intricate patterns made with embroidery-type thread, if the design side of the cloth is the one to be observed, the intertangling of the loops on the back of the piece helps to maintain the stitches in the cloth. In order to retain the integrity of the design and to provide a stopping point for punches, the design should be outlined with needle and regular thread, preferably black (Figure 6-13). This should be the first step after tracing so the design will not erode. For this sort of work I use Corticelli size-50 mercerized thread.

The quickest way to attach the thread to the back of the cloth would be to knot it so it doesn't slip through the cloth. Cotton thread passing through linen, however, will fuzz after a very few stitches and make the outline hazy, so many pieces of thread must be used. If all of these threads were knotted, it would be impossible to punch through them without breaking the outline, leaving a gap, or damaging the needle. You might tack single threads with glue, but you still have to make sure that they are not piled on top of one another but attached individually and away from the design (Figure 6-14).

6-13.

6-14.

The best way to attach the thread is to start each new piece with two or three *back stitches* following the design, leaving the first stitch end hanging free about an inch — this can be snipped off after the second stitch is in. These uncomplicated hanging stitches fasten the thread securely and make it easy to insert the hypo needle without tearing the cloth at the same time. To back stitch, simply stitch backward on each pass of the thread that appears on the surface (Figures 6-15, 6-16, and 6-17).

To clean up lint smears caused by fuzzy thread, form a point of masking tape, sticky side out, and dab the smears with the point. Tweezers will pick up linen filaments as well and roughen the surface of the cloth.

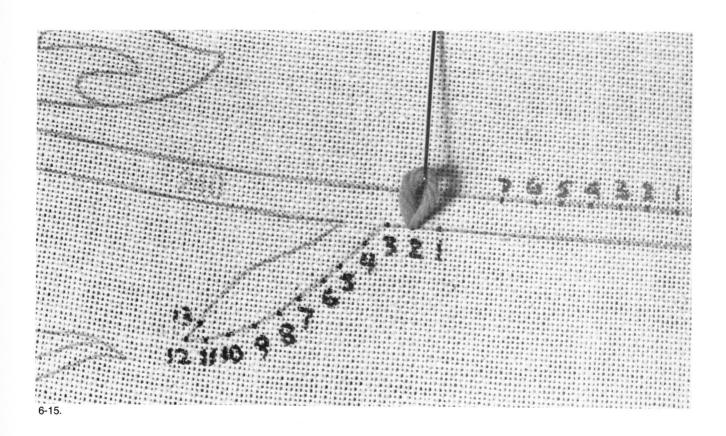

6-15.

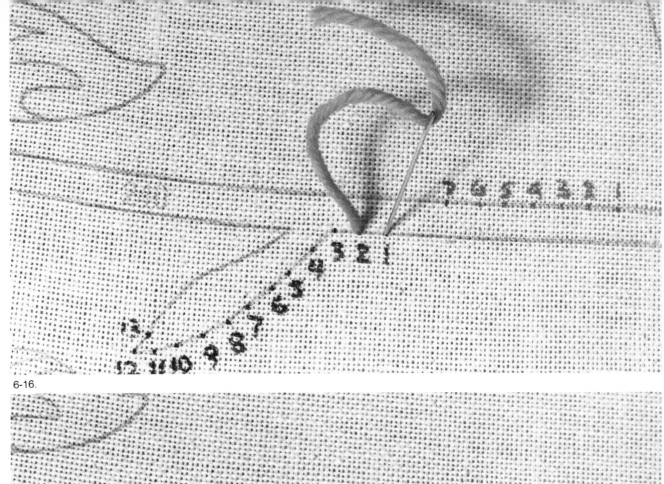

6-16.

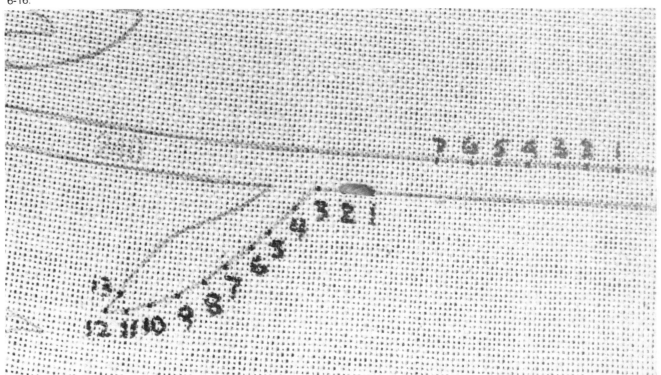

6-17.

CORRECTING MISTAKES

An "authority" is any kind of numbskull who remembers his mistakes. You, too, can be an authority, because if I list 10,000 errors, you will devise others. But at least you will be doing *something* — and a successful endeavor is not one without mistakes but one filled with solutions.

THE BEADING EFFECT

When one line of punches is put into a color mass, it will have the appearance of a row of beads (see the orange line in the branches of the Tree Rug, Figure C-9). If you don't want this effect, two lines of punches will tend to give you an unbroken line of color. If you lack the room in one row, put two stitches in the same distance as for one.

THE UNSAMPLER LOOK

If bias punching is used in curved designs, such as the eagle's wings in the Illeshazy Arms (Figure C-3), a squared-off border will result. To avoid this, use a straight needle, the eye of which is holding two strands (or one less than the hypo) of the same color of thread. From underneath the cloth, come out of the hole containing the last punched stitch — slowly, so as not to dislodge the stitch — and, continuing at a 45-degree angle, that is, on the bias, insert the needle under the border thread. Pull the thread until the two strands are at the same level as the other punches. Do not secure the beginning of this stitch with a knot on the underside of the cloth. Just clip the threads after completing the stitch, leaving the two ends of the thread dangling, since you may want to pick it out from the upper surface with tweezers, which cannot be done with a knot.

You will note that these two-ply stitches will give off a sharper point of light, because they are less than three strands wide and lower in the design than the other stitches. If they bug you, lift them very slightly and press down on the top of the loop with a tine of your tweezers. This will diffuse the sharp point of light.

IRREGULAR PUNCHING AREAS

If your design is too large to be punched without moving it on the frame, there will be some overlapping work areas. The wood of the frame will itself stop your work. If you continue stitching right up to the frame, the last stitches will become somewhat stilted as punching freedom is restricted and, when you change to another position on the frame and resume stitching, you will have one big, homely indentation running across your finished work. Instead, when you begin to approach the frame, punch the border several inches below the wood (or inside any frame that will have to be moved) in an irregular fashion all across the project (Figure 6-18, bottom). When you fill this in on the next installment, you will not have a big, plug-ugly cut running all across your work.

PUNCHED-OUT OR DISPLACED LOOPS

Shoving out a previously made stitch will leave an unsightly, jagged loop on the face of your work. To correct this, hold the displaced loop in the crook of your finger, pull it a bit to give it some tension, slip your scissors below the surface of the work, and snip it out. You won't miss it. Always cut one strand at a time and always cut below the surface, because snipping flush with the surface will leave a dark dot.

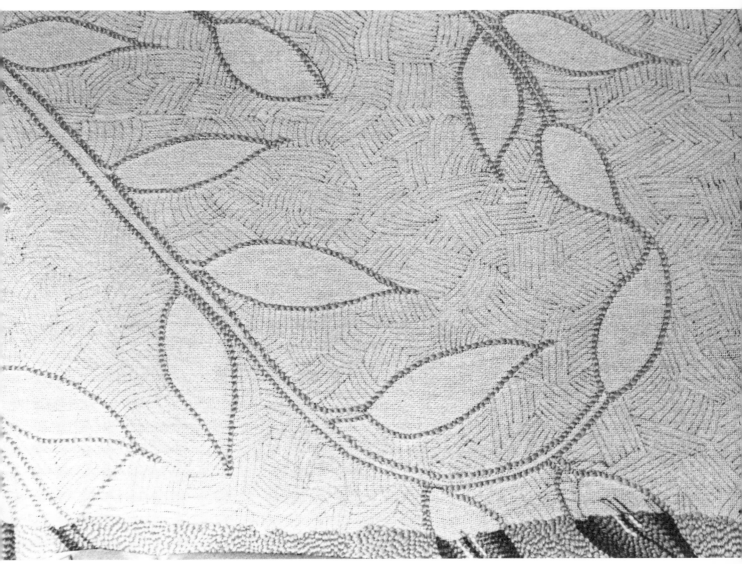

6-18.

HOW TO REDO OR MOVE A DESIGN

Sometimes details of a design will have to be changed. In a map, for example, political lines may have to be moved. At the rate everybody is coming up with his own country, this is a likely prospect. Or you may have to open up a line to allow the name of a place to be lettered. With the gerrymandering going on at this time, I suggest that you try something stable like the South American republics. They only change internally, as a rule.

Anytime you want to move a part of a design, turn the frame over — with the design side up, not the loops — and pull the stitches away from the area in which you wish to rework, allowing at least 2 inches beyond the new design on all sides. Your cloth will be pitted — full of irregular holes from the previous loops. Make the size of the holes uniform as follows:

1. Scratch with your fingernail or the bevel of your needle on the diagonal across the holes — bottom right to top left, bottom left to top right, up, down, and horizontally. With fine cloth like linen, insert a needle into the cloth and make the holes uniform by pushing the warp and weft threads into straight lines.

2. The next little chore is to get the thread or yarn ends back through the cloth. In the case of rug yarn, send the looped piano wire that you used to load the needle (see Chapter 2) through the reverse side from the working face, *loop first*, in the exact spot into which you want the yarn to go. Put the yarn through the loop and snug the end of the loop down to the cloth's surface, leaving a surplus of about ½ to ¾ inch of yarn between the protruding wire loop and the previous stitch. This loop of loose yarn will keep you from pulling out the previous punch. Pressing firmly with a finger on this punch, snap the wire through by pulling it from underneath. If you have pulled this yarn through at the expense of the previous punch, you will have to pull the punch from the cloth, back up one punch, and do it again. To reinsert displaced embroidery thread back into linen, the best way is to stuff the loose thread back through the appropriate hole with a scissors point or needle-nosed, curved tweezers called jewelers' forceps (Figure 6-19). The second-best way is with the two closed points of your iris scissors.

When the cloth is back to its normal shape, sketch in your new design with a felt-tipped pen *on the wrong side only. Do not use these pens on the viewing surface of a design*, especially linen; the ink may run along a thread of the background cloth outside the design area. You may sketch the new design in lightly with a soft, sharp-pointed pencil, but only if that exact line will be covered by thread.

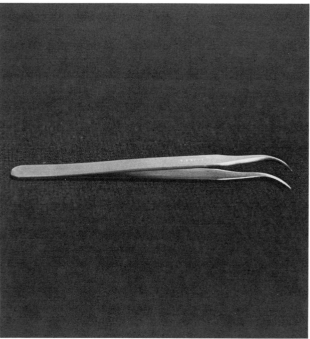

6-19.

THREE-DIMENSIONAL PUNCHERY

When punchery is inserted close together, in a solid front as it were, it looks two-dimensional even though its bulk should make it three-dimensional. To ensure three-dimensionality and the appearance of solidity, you must indicate a light source and subsequent shading away from it. A light source can be indicated by adding highlights to a curved surface. Shading is achieved, as in painting, with gradations of darkness (or lightness) of the same color. This is done by combining varying numbers of differently valued strands of the same color of thread or different intensities of the same or similar hues. This isn't as complicated as it sounds. You just separate the threads as explained in Chapter 2, either in groups of two strands or in single strands, and lay them side by side. You don't have to retwist them; they will be mixed enough by passing through the needle. Put three strands in the needle and punch. In the helmet of the Clopton Arms (Figure C-2), three values of blue plus white were mixed together.

Of course, punching to get a solid effect is done on the bias, as usual. What you have to guard against are abrupt lines of demarcation between two colors or color mixtures, as with the number-painting gems of art from the five-and-ten. To avoid this, alternate the lengths of the diagonal punch lines of each color mix by two or three holes as they approach one another. Dovetail the lines irregularly.

HIGHLIGHTS

If bright, highlighted reflections are desired, such as the white areas on the left-hand side of the Clopton helmet, put in the lightest colors first in the appropriate holes, staggering the lengths of the lines of *diagonal* punches and at the same time following the general contour of the curved surface. Then fill in the darkest border to the left of the highlight and modulate back towards the highlight with gradations of mixed colors. Lastly, fill in the blanks on the diagonals with varying mixtures of tones in between the two extremes of color. To overcome the banded look of a highlight, especially on a surface that diffuses light, such as metal (a reflection on glass would be sharper), single punches of white or a mix of very light shades and white can be sprinkled into the nearby darker mixes.

SHADOWS

Shadows are not as diffused as highlights. They are clear-cut, because they are caused by objects in the path of the light source. A shadow can be indicated by using a darker value of the color on which the light source appears to fall, such as the darker blue below the pendant rope around the neck of the Illeshazy helmet (Figure C-3).

7

All About Maps

The time: 57 B.C.
The place: The English Channel
The Roman ship captain leans against the howling gale and shouts into the first mate's ear, "What shows the napkin?" (In olden times they talked funny.) He wasn't interested at a dire time like this in what the cook had pitched into the stew. (He was in one of his own.) He was asking his mate where he was at (not *where* he was — he knew *where* he was — he was on a sinking trireme out in the English Channel! — but where he was *at*, like at the roag [figure that one out!] or at the end of his life — things like that). Well, back to the napkin. The word "map" comes from *mappa,* which is the Latin word for "napkin." (I guess he was speaking Latin, but you never know, what with all those expensive wars of Caesar's and with the union and all — he may have been a Panamanian.) Anyhow, just like *charta* is Latin for "papyrus" or "parchment," delineated navigational aids, such as sea routes and land masses, were named for material they were on.

DIFFERENT KINDS OF MAPS

There are maps aplenty to trace, from the minutest details to the broadest recognizable contours. You can use all of your creative urges to show off your own piece of real estate. Maps can be mere profiles or they can be intricately lettered, as there are many intriguing devices to show subject matter.

INSET MAPS

Suppose you want to show the island of Taiwan. You can show a small, monotone-gray map of Taiwan inside a rectangle that encompasses the coast of China, *Time* or *Newsweek* style. A detailed map, which would be an enlargement of the gray sector, would show the island. Both maps would be within the same frame (Figure 7-1). The fact that the small map overlapped the larger map would indicate the correspondence between the two.

WIDE-ANGLE MAPS

Figures C-7 and C-5 are reproductions of maps of the British Isles and Europe showing my son's grand-tour route. I call these "wide-angle" maps, because there is quite a lot of territory that has nothing to do with the subject but has a lot to do with the design of the map. Putting in the northeastern and southeastern ramparts of Europe not only completed the design but made the trip look more extensive. By including the northern coast of Africa, although it was not too important to the trip, the spectacular Italian Peninsula was dramatized, the Mediterranean Sea was able to be shown complete, and the picture was given a bottom land mass to contain the water. Having a body of water pour off or out of the picture weakens a design, and besides, it's liable to ruin the rug.

7-1. Inset map of Taiwan by Warren Bredlow.

FINELY DETAILED MAPS

Maps can go into the greatest detail, even delineating indentations in a battlement wall of a city (Figure 7-2), a group of harbors (Figure 7-3), or a group of islands (Figure 7-4). These are drawn maps that allow for a great amount of detail.

Stitchery can indicate great detail also, as the map of Mexico shows (Figure C-4). The Gulf of Mexico was made interesting (and is it bare!) by extending the names of Texas coastal cities into it. The Gulf itself is closed up by the Florida Keys, the Tortugas, and Cuba, so it won't leak off the edge. It was possible to complete Florida, but that would divert the eye from the center of interest, Mexico. The Mexican portion of the Yucatan Peninsula could not very well have been shown without completing Central America, which avoids an unlikely land amputation and also helps to contain the gulf. This map was designed to focus attention on the routes of different trips and places of archaeological interest.

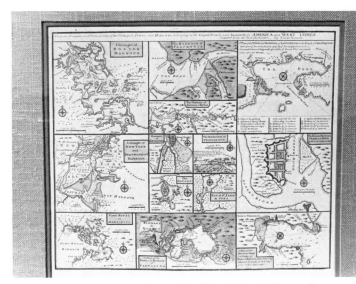

7-3. Map of harbors in America and the West Indies by Emanuel Bowen. (Courtesy of George M. Illes)

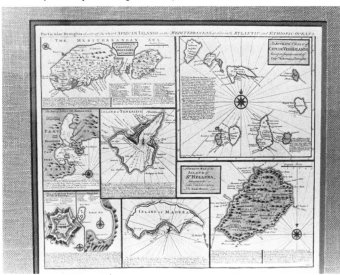

7-4. Map of African islands in the Mediterranean, Atlantic, and Ethiopic Oceans by Emanuel Bowen. (Courtesy of George M. Illes)

7-2. Map of city fortifications in the state of Lombardy by Cornelis Danckerts. (Courtesy of George M. Illes)

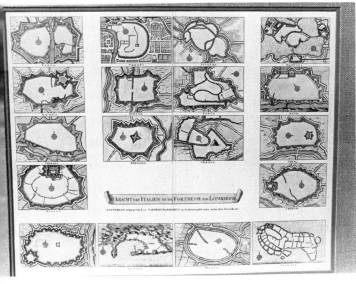

CARTOUCHES

The ornate devices engraved in the corners of ancient maps that exhibit the scale of miles, the points of the compass, and other pertinent information are called *cartouches* (Figures 7-5 and 7-6). These not only vented the artistic fires smoldering in the engraver's scientific soul but also were his hallmark against counterfeiting. A cartographer's reputation kept his head and shoulders joined. An improper map could mean a dynasty's demise when a battle won or lost settled the next 100-years' hash. Cartographers were often so jealously guarded by their benefactors that, like alchemists, some were imprisoned for life. But with the knowledge the mapsters had of the royal real estate, their princely benefactors, while turning the keys in their dungeon locks, were trying to avoid that political sport now called "Leaking Secrets." (By the way, what do they use the basement of the Capitol Building for?)

Milliare Germanicum commune.
500   1000   1500   2000

Schale van 2000 Blorsche Roeden maeckende een gemeene
Duytsche Myle van 15 in een graedt.

t'Nieuwe diep

t'Nieuwe

t'Velt   San

Den Banjaert
aen alle syde Steyl

Querens   Vierboet   Breezant   t'Vel

COMITATUS ZELANDIÆ TABULA
emendata a FREDERICO DE WIT amstelodami.

7-5 and 7-6. Seventeenth-century map of the Walcheren Islands by
Federico de Wit. The detail shows the cartouche.

For you, stitching in a cartouche might not be physically unsafe, but working its intricacies might well prove to be a devastating emotional experience, although ornate map stitchery has been done before (Figures 7-7 and 7-8).

7-7. Nineteenth-century cross-stitched map of England by Ann Gardiner. (Courtesy of the Victoria and Albert Museum)

7-8. Nineteenth-century map of the world in satin and chain stitches. (Courtesy of the Victoria and Albert Museum)

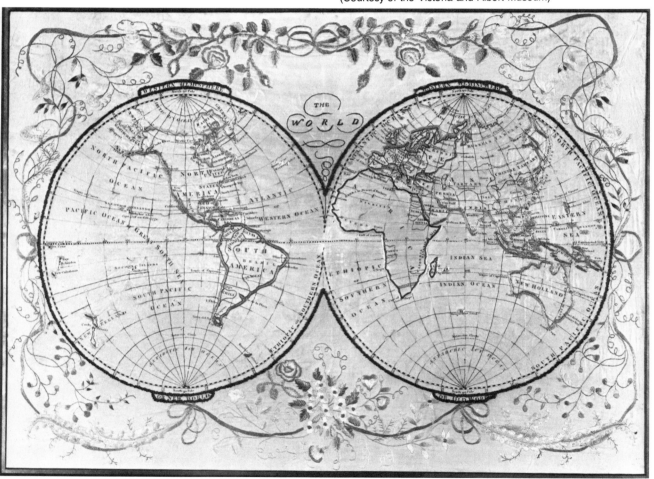

VARYING THE SIZE OF MAPS

It is practically impossible to enlarge or decrease the size of a map by the grid-transfer route. Coastlines are far too complex to transfer, no matter how many points of reference you put on your small-scale or large-scale grid. Then how do you decrease or increase the size of a map? With a big Xerox machine. Blueprint firms have big duplicating machines. You can start with any size and end with any size, large or small. I would suggest that you get several copies. (I must say that it is cheaper to satisfy yourself with maps already available from the American Automobile Association, tourist bureaus of foreign countries, or travel agents.)

MIXING COLORS IN MAPS

As I said in Chapter 5, when two differently colored threads are placed side by side, each will influence the color of the other. Threads that look fetching side by side in skeins may not be so appealing when they are strung out in narrow lines of punches and stitches, which do not have the same reflective power as a thick bundle of threads in a skein. To know how one color will affect its neighbor, trial lines of colors should be punched outside of your design area, not in straight lines but in convoluted curves, to see how they will live together. There are six different nations whose borders lie adjacent to that of Austria, for example (Figure C-6). To find six different colors compatible with Austria's border and with each other makes its color selection as complicated as its politics. If an exceptionally strong color tends to overpower a neighboring one, the balance can be restored by dropping one row of the strong color. This was done with the strong red color of East Germany. One row of red was enough.

Of all of the world's cartographic and physical attributes, its coastlines offer the most exciting lines to play with: their arms, inlets, and curvaceous beaches are littorally breathtaking, as are their prominences, both rock-bound and bikini-clad. Coastlines are most effective when they are stitched with several graded colors side by side, so they offer great opportunities for color interplay. For instance, the coasts of England and Mexico both use three blue colors to delineate the line of the sea as it joins the land. There is no reason why colors other than blue cannot be used, but the number of rows of different colors depends solely on the space available. Sometimes there is no way to tuck more than two rows of colors into lagoons, bays, or inlets, or between coast-hugging islands and the mainland. Anyhow, two rows of fairly divergent tones of one color will make a reasonable color gradation, since, according to our law, two colors lying close together will affect each other, giving the appearance of more than just two. Only two colors were used in portions of the western Scottish islands, the western Irish islands, the Dalmatian Islands on the west coast of Yugoslavia, and the islands off the Central American coast, but it looks like more. Too many rows of colors around tiny islands make them look like carbuncles. There is no need to stint; considering all the wild and wooly threads and yarns of today, you can just about tie on a big color binge.

TRANSFERRING A MAP TO CLOTH

It is more difficult to trace a map than the simpler designs discussed in Chapter 4, so here are some additional suggestions. A mattress board large enough to extend beyond all four sides of the total map design is very helpful.

    1. Lay the mattress board on a table. If you are going to work on your friends' fine-surfaced dining-room table, place a quilt or blanket under the board to protect the table (Figure 7-9). Place several layers of newspaper on the mattress board for sponginess and tape them to the board (Figure 7-10). Try to avoid deep creases between the sections of the paper. You can tape wax paper over the newspaper, as newsprint will dirty your cloth. If you make an error on one side, you can turn the cloth over and use the other side, but not if it is smeared with ink.

7-9.

7-10.

2. Stretch the cloth and tape it to the board — not to the table — to get some tension on the cloth (Figure 7-11). Be sure that one warp thread and one weft thread coincide with the edge of the mattress board along its total length and width. This ensures that your design will be truly perpendicular (check this with a T-square — Figure 7-12) and, if you have any lettering to do, it will come out truly horizontal along the weft-thread lines.

3. Run a strip of masking tape around the perimeter of the cloth close to the edge (Figure 7-13).

4. Cut a single piece of carbon paper and attach it to the background cloth by fastening it to the strip of masking tape (Figure 7-14). Make sure that the carbon paper does not crease or bunch, as the slightest pressure will transfer that ripple onto the cloth.

5. Attach the design to the masking tape. Make sure that the design coincides perpendicularly and horizontally with the cloth (Figure 7-15).

6. With a large map for which the cloth adjacent to the carbon is to be the face of your project, take great care not to transfer any carbon to the cloth, as it just cannot be cleaned off — the whole thing would have to be done over again on another piece of cloth. I place my tracing arm and elbow on a soft, flat pillow, itself placed on the design, so that this pressure will not transfer a smudge (Figure 7-16).

7-11.

7-12.

92

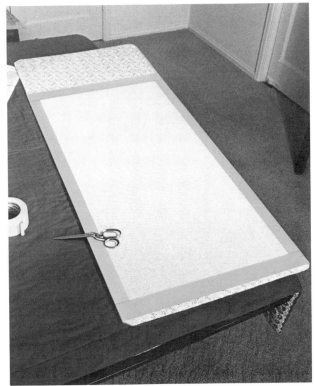

7-13.

7-15.

7-14.

7-16.

7. Trace your design by perforating it with a superhard, sharp, lead pencil (Figure 7-17). Do not be alarmed if the pencil perforates the mattress board, but remember that the farther it penetrates, the larger that dot will be. Quite a bit of detail can be transferred without punching into the mattress board at all.

8. When you have finished tracing, release three sides of your masking tape down to the cloth level. Carefully lift the released layers, including the carbon, and compare your design with what you have traced to see if all of the details have been reproduced. If you have missed something, lower the carbon carefully and secure it to the cloth; then lower the design and resecure it before doing any more transferring. Again, use the pillow. A slip of the carbon at this point will leave a blue blur on your material that cannot be eradicated.

9. When you are satisfied that you are finished, carefully lift off the pattern and the carbon. Leave the cloth secured to the mattress board, take it all outside, set it up vertically against something solid, and spray your design at least three times with a thin plastic coat, allowing several minutes between sprayings. This ensures that the carbon's waxy ink will not smudge the cloth as you work around your design.

7-17.

Tracing a map, like studying for an exam, is a very personal exercise. Since you cannot possibly trace all of the detail onto the cloth, you must make up your own code with little marks and punches. You will develop your own signals to advise you when to take a good, close squint at the map itself. And from the map, not from your tracings, you will form your bay, island, delta, or roag (if you ever find out what this is). All I can tell you is how to get fixed up so you can start for yourself.

Trace your map in such a position that your lettering lines will be horizontal. I can guarantee that trying to make letters on a curve or slanting across the threads is just plain hell. Two examples, which are by no means perfect but which are the results of many take-outs and put-ins and a lot of crying, are the names Adriatic and Hungary in the Europe map. The time will come when you cannot avoid this dilemma. I can't help you; I can only offer you my heartfelt sympathy. One way to escape this situation is to avoid maps in which the curvature of the earth is highly accentuated. The countries at the upper left- and right-hand corners will invariably fly off at weirdo angles.

The best method that I have found for tracing a map is to make a series of punches along the borders and other pertinent lines, such as rivers and routes, with a hard-lead, sharp-pointed pencil. After you have punched a series of dots into the map and cloth, let it go at that; do not go over the dots. If you missed any, you will pick them up when you inspect your cloth. Continual punching in one spot will give you an unsightly blob.

The spots for towns, cities, and other points should be traced very lightly. The lettering for the names of towns, cities, oceans, rivers, bays, and roags should *never, under any circumstances,* be traced in. The lettering will have to be jockeyed to fit in with a lot of other stitched lines and may fall above, below, left, right, or maybe not on the map at all. There is no telling where the name will end up. As the carbon cannot be erased from the cloth, I reiterate — *trace no lettering.*

If you plan to put in a cartouche, don't trace in a bunch of fuzzy lines for the characters. Unerasable carbon-paper lines will ruin your cloth.

FRENCH KNOTS

I designate mountains on my maps with +s; archaeological sites, with ▲s; and cities, with French knots — different colors to distinguish between capitals and other cities. I have never read a concise description of making a French knot, and I'm not going to try to turn the tide here. Any embroidery shop will have some nice, kindly lady who will show you how to make them. One thing is certain — with all the activity and cloth vibration going on in punching, these knots, unless they are anchored, will end up looking like *Fantasia* worms peering out of their holes.

After you have made the standard French knot, come back through the cloth from the underside, on the side of the knot away from the first stitch, and push the needle back down through the center of the rosette of the knot. Pull this thread through slowly until the second loop, which will form over the rim of the knot, has the same tension as the first. You can tell when this is reached, because any additional pull will tilt the rosette. Clip this second thread under the cloth and tack it with glue.

LETTERING

HOW TO LOCATE THE POSITIONS OF NAMES ON MAPS

Each place has a name, and each name has a certain number of letters separated by spaces. In N-E-B-R-A-S-K-A, for example, there are eight letters and seven spaces. In map stitchery, the letters and spaces are thought of in terms of holes — meaning the gaps between the warp and weft threads. The best place to put a state's name is approximately in the middle of the state from left to right and a little higher than the middle when measuring from top to bottom; in general, a name should be roughly equidistant from the bulk of the left and right borders and slightly nearer to the bulk of the top than to the bottom border.

To center a name in a given area, do the following:

1. Count the number of holes from the left border to the right border. In our example, for purposes of demonstration, let us say that Nebraska contains seventy-five holes between the left border and the right border.

2. Allowing, in this instance, three holes for each letter and one hole for each space, depicted by a hyphen, N-E-B-R-A-S-K-A needs twenty-four holes for the letters and seven for the hyphens, or thirty-one holes altogether.

3. To center thirty-one holes within seventy-five holes in the width of the state, subtract thirty-one from seventy-five, which is forty-four. Divide the forty-four by two, and lo! you get twenty-two. The left-hand element of the beginning letter N is started at the twenty-second hole from the left border.

4. Assuming that Nebraska has thirty-six holes from the top of the state line to the bottom and that the letters are square, that is, three holes wide and three holes high, thirty-six less three equals thirty-three holes; as close as you can come in dividing thirty-one by two (you can't split a hole) is sixteen and seventeen. By putting the name slightly above the center of the vertical space, the top left-hand point of the first letter will be sixteen holes from the top border and twenty-two holes from the left-hand border. This is the starting point for lettering N-E-B-R-A-S-K-A.

5. Before you start stitching, count out thirty-one holes, beginning at the starting point, to make sure that they are (a) equidistant and (b) appear proper in the allotted space. If the name looks pinched in the middle of the state area, you can widen it by adding some of the forty-four outside holes (twenty-two on each end of N-E-B-R-A-S-K-A) to the spaces between the letters. Say that you add two holes to each space, making a total of fourteen; adding these to the thirty-one of the present width results in forty-five. Subtract this from the total of seventy-five to get thirty holes, or fifteen holes away from each border. The distance from the top and bottom will remain the same.

Some places are not even remotely rectangular in shape like Nebraska. To center a name in such cases, experiment with your pointed bow (Figure 4-15) at various widths to determine where you think the name should be. This depends solely on what looks best to you. I used the bow method to place all of the names in all of the maps shown in this book.

PLANNING LETTER SIZES

Some things are in good taste and some things are not. Certain incongruous letter sizes will overpower an otherwise poetic impression. To announce the birth of your six-pound heiress, you wouldn't use thirty-point Bodoni (not the odds in the third race but a size and style of type), and bold Gothic type wouldn't look good on a wedding announcement, no matter how happy they were to get her married off.

All of the names of places in one country and of countries in one continent should be the same size. In a double name like New York, make the distance between the first and second name twice the distance between the letters themselves. Bodies of water and land areas can be distinguished when they both appear in the body of water by italicizing either the water names or the land names. Italics require less space than vertical letters, but the height remains the same. To try to letter the names of rivers along the squiggly lines, as tiny as they must be, will require patience, a calm disposition, and a full array of tranquilizers.

The size of lettering can be greatly reduced by using silk thread. After stitching two or three letters with silk thread, secure the thread with glue, then cut it before starting another series of letters. If you clip silk thread before it is secured, it may slip out of the cloth. Cotton and linen shrink and expand with humidity, while silk does not. Long strands of silk strung across linen or cotton will either pucker the cloth along the line of lettering or the lettering will disappear under the folds of the warp and weft thread crossings.

One of the best explanations of letter form and spacing is the *Speedball Textbook for Pen and Brush Lettering* by George F. Ross, which is obtainable at art supply stores. Many beautiful ancient and modern print styles are shown, and, although it is designed for pen and brush, its demonstrations of letter spacing apply to stitchery as well. Some of the exotic letter styles would be fascinating in thread.

As shown on page 91 of the *Speedball* book, mechanical separation of letters can make a word look as if it were chopped up into piles. If you find that you are suffering from piles, take out the letter that offends and move it (see below). *Mechanical separation* in our stitchery sense means separating letters by equal numbers of spaces created by the warp and weft threads between each letter. With the square letters in basic Gothic, which I recommend that you use, mechanical separation will work most of the time in stitchery. However, there are certain letter combinations that will have to be adjusted to maintain uniform tension between the letters and to prevent having one lost little sheep off all by itself. There is a feeling of blankness between an L and a following A, and a confusion results when a P or an F follows too closely after an I or a J after an A, so variations in the mechanical separation will have to be made, and you will have to eyeball the distance.

HOW TO FORM THE LETTERS

Figure 7-18 shows the formation of each letter in punch stitchery. The arrows point in the direction that the stitch should go. It is always better to push into a hole that contains a thread rather than pulling a thread out through an occupied hole, because you might dislodge the previous thread.

The following letters do not require any special attention to keep them full-sized or to cover the chosen height of two or more weft threads: B, C, D, E, G, O, Q, S, and Z. Each of these letters is formed with a horizontal arm or element in both the upper and the lower horizontal positions of the letter so that any shortness of the verticals is filled in by the thickness of the horizontals. Apart from what can be added for decoration, a C, for instance, is made up of three elements: an upper horizontal, a vertical, and a lower horizontal; an O has an upper and a lower horizontal and two verticals; an E has one vertical and three horizontals, and so on.

Into your test piece of linen put a vertical thread spanning two horizontal threads, such as the vertical in the letter C. You will note that the stress put on the thread at the bottom of the upper hole and at the top of the bottom hole causes the thread to look short (and it is) — shorter than the completed letter with the upper and lower horizontals attached. But it becomes full height with the addition of the horizontals.

Now, each of the letters A, F, H, I, J, K, L, M, N, P, R, T, U, V, W, and Y lacks one or both of the horizontal elements, such as at the top of the vertical element in the letter L. To ensure that the ends of the free-standing vertical elements don't become too short by sneaking off to the inner edges of their holes, they must be anchored by passing the thread of that element a few filaments higher or lower into the next horizontal thread immediately above or below the normal habitation area. I have termed these stitches *filament stitches*.

A *working hole* is a hole into which or from which a thread of an element of a letter enters or emerges. In Figure 7-18 stitches depicted by arrows begin and end at a working hole. Stitches shown in this way are regular stitches in and out of working holes. Stitches that appear to lie on top of a horizontal thread begin as filament stitches, that is, the stitch begins or ends a tiny amount into the horizontal thread above or below the working hole. The bottom of the vertical stitch of the letter F, for instance, appears to go below the normal working hole for that stitch. It goes a few filaments deep into the next lower horizontal thread.

7-18. Formation of Gothic letters in punch stitchery. Background by Marie Loos; stitches by Warren Bredlow.

The filament stitches for asymmetric letters are the following: A at all three points; F at the lower end of the vertical; H at both ends of both verticals; I at both ends of the vertical; J at the top of the vertical; K at both ends of the vertical and at both ends of the angles; L at the top of the vertical; M at the top and bottom of both verticals and at the bottom of the V formed between the verticals; N at the top and bottom of both verticals; P at the bottom of the vertical; R at the bottom of the left vertical and at the bottom of the right-hand angle; T at the bottom of the vertical; U at the tops of both verticals; V at the tops and bottoms of both stitches; W at the tops and bottoms of both sides and at the peak at the top of the inverted V — like M in reverse; and Y at the bottom of the lower-half vertical and at the tops of the two angles. Each one of those points invades the horizontal nearest its normal working hole.

The above instructions relate to letters whose verticals are perpendicular to the weft threads. To ensure the parallelism of so-called vertical lines in italics, which are at a slant rather than perpendicular as in rectangular lettering, and to control their spacing, the same general rules apply as for perpendicular verticals. If it appears that one end of an italicized vertical will have to be inserted or exserted in the center of a background-cloth warp or weft thread in order to be parallel to its companion's italicized vertical, such as the second vertical in the letter N with the first, come out of the cloth from beneath at the desired distance from either the top or the bottom of the first vertical and pull the needle and thread until all of it is above the cloth. Then, picking up the thread in the hand that you are not stitching with, line up the thread by eyeballing it (visually paralleling it with the first) and insert the needle into the cloth directly under the held thread at the prescribed point to be the same height as the first vertical (Figure 7-19). This will give you an italicized vertical which is parallel to your first vertical. If you try to make a short stitch without first paralleling it with its companion, the chances are that you will have a crippled-looking letter on your hands.

7-19. Formation of Gothic italics in punch stitchery. Background by Marie Loos; stitches by Warren Bredlow.

HOW TO REMOVE A RECALCITRANT LETTER

Letters in stitchery can exhibit wild eccentricities or be invaded by voodoo devils. If one letter in a word, through shrinkage or other undue tension, is too light in color, stunted in size, or badly spaced, anchor the other letters on either side of the miscreant letter with tacky glue and remove the recalcitrant letter by snipping its stitches on the back of the cloth and extracting the letter with your tweezers from the front (working side) of the cloth. If there seems to be a smudge of color on the cloth, do not blow your stack — this is merely lint, and it can be removed by touching it with the sticky side of masking tape.

MATTING

If you decide to use a mat, the rule, regardless of the size of your map, is: the bottom must be ⅝ inch wider than the other three sides.

If you are dissatisfied with the spark and verve of your colors, gloom not. You can pick up any of them with a green matting, because green is complementary to all of the reds and the analogous yellows and oranges. If green turns you off or clashes with your room, then go to a gray tone of one of the vibrant shades used for a small area in your map. Do not use purples or dark blues, as they die at night.

No matter what size map you make, there will be a point where a land border will have to be cut. Bring your mat right up to that terminal point of the stitchery; do not mat outside of that point, or the cut will look like the place where the ancients fell off the flat earth.

A plain frame should be used; let the mat do your sparking. Stay away from glare-proof and windowpane glass; these will ruin your labors. Use Plexiglas instead; even though it is 8 to 10 percent more expensive than the other glasses, it is absolutely marvelous.

8

Large Projects

THE ADJUSTABLE FRAME

An adjustable frame is one in which the pieces of wood onto which the background cloth is attached float free and inside of a rigid outer frame, to which they are attached only by threaded bolts. This allows tension to be applied to the inner frame by simply tightening the bolts. There are two good reasons for having an adjustable frame that can be tightened or loosened mechanically:

1. With large and bulky projects, such as rugs or wall hangings, the adjustable frame makes it possible to get sufficient tension on the cloth. Larger working areas require more pull at the side of the frame than smaller areas, because the pull at the frame's edge is diluted by the number of square inches in the working area. For instance, in a frame 5 inches by 6 inches, sufficient tension can be obtained by grasping the cloth by hand before stapling (see Chapter 3). But the same amount of pull would not tighten a cloth 5 feet by 6 feet sufficiently for it to be punched. The center of the larger cloth would have the tension of a butt-sprung hammock. The farther you get from the frame's edge, the less the tension is.

2. With smaller projects, the adjustable frame can be used to increase and decrease the tension of unsynthetic cloths such as linen, which loosen or tighten with changing humidity. Moreover, the smaller the project, the smaller the stitches tend to be, and a finer-woven background cloth should be used. Smaller stitches can only be made by using smaller needles and finer thread, and the smaller the needle, the more critical the uniformity of the tension becomes. Uniformity of tension helps to ensure uniformly sized stitches. To maintain uniformity of tension with a static frame, you often have to pull the staples, retighten the cloth by hand or with canvas pliers (Figure 3-19, right), and restaple it. Excessive stapling endangers the cloth, especially the finer weaves, so a frame that allows instant adjustment of tension without restapling is of great importance to your project and your equanimity.

Figure 8-1 shows a simple, schematic sketch of an adjustable frame. You can get it all together in an afternoon with a saw and a drill and a modicum of charged language. The black bars represent the adjustable, floating frame, to which the cloth can be easily attached with staples. The outer, white frame in this case is static. The frame can also be made extendable, as shown in Figure 8-2. The bolts with nuts represented in this drawing are ¼-inch threaded rods. The outer frame should be made of some rather firm wood (2 inches by 2 inches), and the inner ones (black) should be made out of soft wood, such as white pine, for easy stapling. Washers are to be used next to the wood wherever pressure is applied. Regular hex nuts should be used on both ends of the threaded rods. For tightening the hex nuts, use a ratcheted box wrench with a $^7/_{16}$-inch box on one end (Figure 8-3).

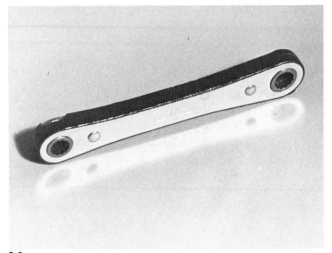

8-3.

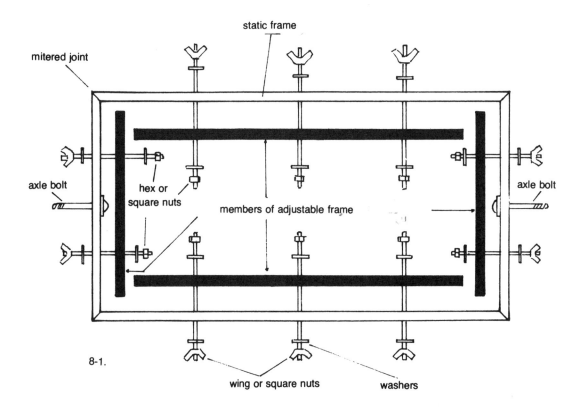

8-1.

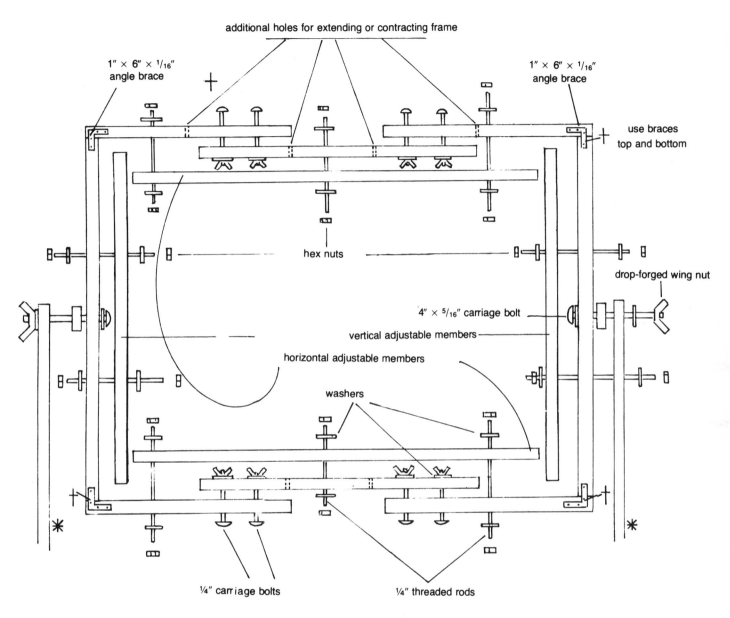

additional holes for extending or contracting frame

1″ × 6″ × 1/16″
angle brace

1″ × 6″ × 1/16″
angle brace

use braces
top and bottom

hex nuts

drop-forged wing nut

4″ × 5/16″ carriage bolt

vertical adjustable members

horizontal adjustable members

washers

1/4″ carriage bolts

1/4″ threaded rods

*uprights of the
stand

†flat-angle braces may be used here

use bracers on both sides

8-2.

Don't be alarmed at the seeming chaos of the exploded view of the adjustable frame (Figure 8-4). Everything fits and has a purpose, which is to control the width of the working surface, thus reducing the movement of the cloth. Each time the cloth is moved and stapled, there is a chance of damaging it.

The width of the frame can be extended and contracted in the same manner as the width of the stand (see below). You will notice additional holes along the three-pieced horizontal sides of the static portion of the frame for moving the pieces laterally.

There are four pieces of wood that will have to be changed with each change in width of the project. Figure 8-5 shows two of them, the dowels upon which the excess cloth is wound and the other horizontal members of the adjustable, floating, inner frame as seen in Figure 8-2. The attachment of vertical dowel holders is shown in Figures 8-6 and 8-7.

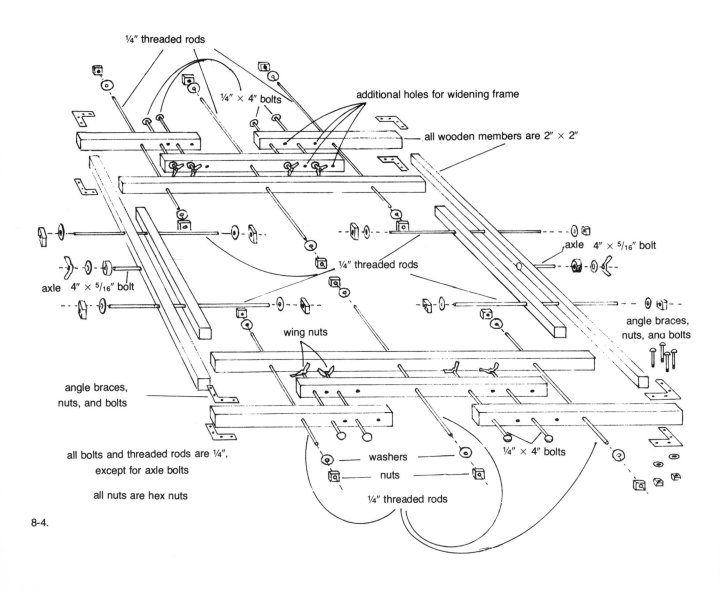

¼" threaded rods

¼" × 4" bolts

additional holes for widening frame

all wooden members are 2" × 2"

axle 4" × ⁵/₁₆" bolt

¼" threaded rods

axle 4" × ⁵/₁₆" bolt

angle braces, nuts, and bolts

wing nuts

angle braces, nuts, and bolts

¼" × 4" bolts

all bolts and threaded rods are ¼", except for axle bolts

washers

nuts

all nuts are hex nuts

¼" threaded rods

8-4.

8-5.

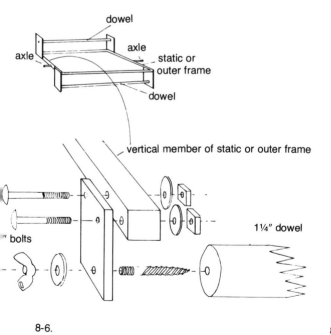

dowel

axle

axle

static or
outer frame

dowel

vertical member of static or outer frame

" bolts

1¼" dowel

8-6.

8-7.

THE ADJUSTABLE STAND

Figure 8-8 shows how to construct an adjustable stand. All of the wooden members, including the feet, are made with 1-inch-by-5-inch lumber.

Slots are used in the base so that the width of the stand can easily be expanded or contracted to accommodate the width of the frame. The wider the stand is stretched, the more you will have to brace it. That is the reason for the plate under the midjoint of the center section of the base. It may also be necessary to attach 8-inch straight braces at a 45-degree angle between the uprights and the parts of the base with the slots (Figure 8-9). The straight braces stay attached while the frame and stand are used, but they can be removed to fold the stand for storing. They afford additional rigidity of the uprights, which helps to stabilize the whole operation. Screen-door braces should also be added between the upright and the feet to give vertical support (Figure 8-10).

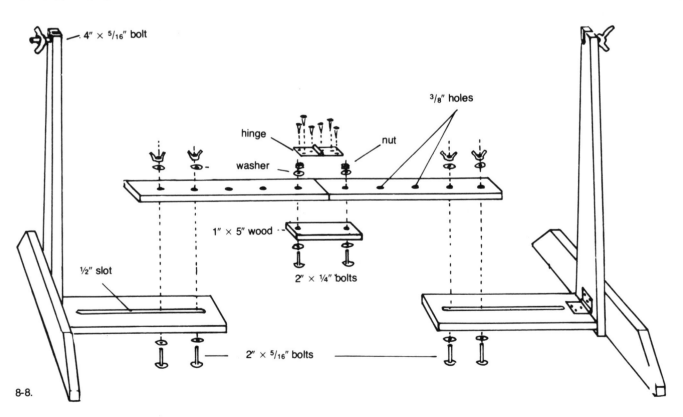

8-8.

8-9.

8-10.

8-11.

4" × 5/16"
bolt

1½" × 1⅛"

——— 1⅛" ———
cross section
of
rectangular
frame

—½"—
dowel
in diameter

¾"

upright
1" × 5"
white
or ponderosa
pine

washer

wing nut 5/16"
drop-forged
(not cast)

DETAIL AT THE AXLE OF THE FRAME

THE INTERNAL BRACE

You may notice that the horizontal rigid-frame bars sag from tension, especially with a wide 6-foot or 7-foot project. Figure 8-12 shows an internal, vertical brace that you can make and attach that will alleviate a lot of sag. You can use the midpoint-threaded rods along the horizontal bars of the rigid frame to keep the crossbar from slipping out sideways (Figure 8-4). Or you can drill separate holes close to the midpoints of each horizontal bar, bolt the brace separately, and fasten it to the horizontal members of the rigid frame. Without bolting, the brace could conceivably squirt out under pressure and go flying off across the room. Here's how to do it:

1. Measure the inside distance between the horizontal elements of the rigid frame. Cut a 2-inch-by-2-inch bar exactly that length.

2. Buy two L-braces of the plain 5-inch-by-6-inch, shelf-bracket type from a hardware store. These braces must hold terrific pressure, so they will have to be sturdy. If you don't have a metal drill, have the hardware-store people drill two holes for you, one in each side of the long arm of the brace close to the elbow.

3. Using $3/16$-inch or $1/4$-inch bolts, attach this brace as shown in Figure 8-12. (Bolts are necessary, as screws will tear out of the wood as the pressure builds up.) Also have your hardware man drill a hole wide enough at the end of each short arm of the L-brace so that you can slip a $1/4$-inch bolt through.

4. Release the tension on the horizontal bars of the adjustable frame and slip the internal brace in so that the exposed ends of the L-braces are between the inside faces of the rigid-frame bars (Figure 8-12). Attach the internal brace with bolts to the frame — this is why it is better to have separate holes for these bolts — so that you can put the brace in and take it out without messing around with the long, threaded bar that is used for tension. Now repull your tension along the horizontal adjustable-frame bars.

HOW TO ENLARGE THE SIZE OF A CLOTH

For a big project, the cloth that you use should extend at least 8 inches beyond your pattern on all sides. You may have to join two pieces of cloth together to make the background large enough for your purpose. All woven material has specially finished edges along the length of the cloth to prevent raveling. These are called *selvages*. The two pieces of cloth you wish to join should be stitched along the inner edge of the selvage, which affords you a straight guideline that won't unravel $1/4$ inch from the edge of the cloth.

Place one selvage on top of the other and machine stitch down the inside of the selvage line along the whole length of your joining. At the ends of the joining you should backstitch or doublestitch about 1 inch to prevent loosening. This joining should be completed before you start the two rows of stitching to avoid raveling around the perimeter.

If you wish to join two pieces of cloth that have no selvage, you can make your own. Pull a thread along one side of each of the two pieces to act as guidelines and sew as if you had selvage. Whether you are dealing with factory or with your own pulled-line homemade selvage, press the seam between the two pieces of cloth with an iron after either has been stitched.

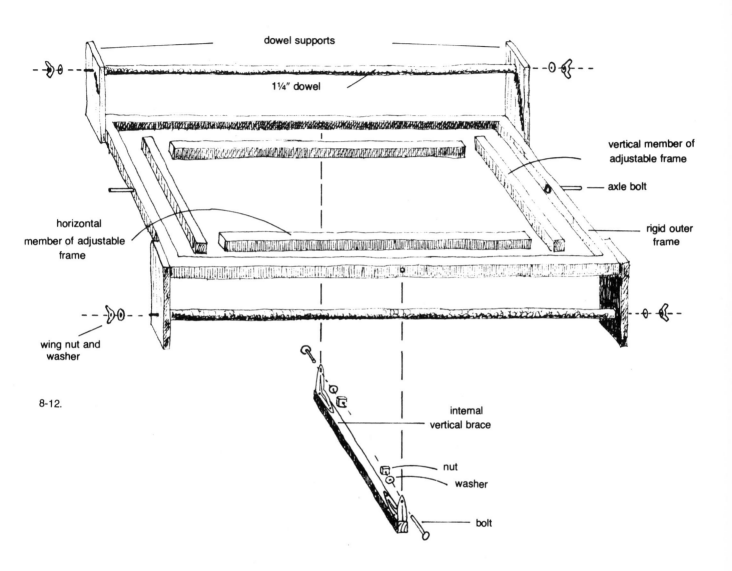

dowel supports

1¼" dowel

vertical member of
adjustable frame

axle bolt

rigid outer
frame

horizontal
member of adjustable
frame

wing nut and
washer

8-12.

internal
vertical brace

nut

washer

bolt

BATHROOM RUGS

In times of dubious energy supply, if you are sick and tired of having your feet cold all the way up to behind your ears when you step onto a bare floor of a morning, one large project you might whip up is a wall-to-wall bathroom rug. Although we might harness the sun's rays before you finish it, here is how to start the rug.

MAKING A CORRUGATED RUG PATTERN

In making a wall-to-wall rug, you are not only involved in transferring the internal design but also in adhering to the exact outline of the room's perimeter, complete with moldings, closets, doors, cabinets, French windows, or other floor/wall indentations. A rug for a powder room or bathroom must also take into account the bathtub and the john pedestal. To render the detail of the indentations correctly, a contour gauge (Figure 8-13) should be used.

If the room is completely asymmetrical, such as the powder room that the Bird Rug (Figure C-10) was made for, the proper outline can be ensured if you fit together a pattern made out of pieces of corrugated paper, including the base of the john pedestal, and actually lay it down on the floor and tape it together with masking tape. After a complete cardboard carpet has been taped together, cut a slit in the cardboard, preferably at the back of the john, and remove the pattern from the pedestal intact; then retape the slit to form the john-pedestal opening. This corrugated profile can then be used to trace the border, with the pedestal slot in its actual position, onto your to-be-gridded paper pattern and also onto your piece of background cloth.

8-13.

TRANSFERRING LARGE DESIGNS

In transferring large designs, a grid is very important. The best way to make a large grid for a project with strict measurements is to obtain a strip of lightweight plywood in the desired width from the lumberyard.

1. To figure the proper width of the plywood strip, use the small design that you have already traced on graph or grid paper. Count the number of squares (not the lines) on this paper that encompass your design; you will need the same number of squares on your big-sized grid. If your rug is to be 7¼ feet by 6¼ feet, for example, and each square on the small grid paper is ⅛ inch square, multiply the number of spaces both vertically and horizontally by ninety-six — the number of ⅛ inches in 1 foot — to get 696/8 inches × 600/8 inches. Assuming again that there are fifteen squares per inch on your graph paper, divide the width measurement (600/8) by fifteen to get 40/8 inches, or 5 inches, which is the width that each of the squares on the large grid and your strip of plywood should be.

2. Now lay your corrugated-paper design (if it is a wall-to-wall rug) on top of a piece of laundry paper (or strips joined together) large enough for the full-sized design and place both of these on a hard surface, such as the kitchen floor. If your kitchen is smaller than your desired rug size plus 3 feet on all sides for kneeling room, use a concrete tennis court — but not on a windy day. Trace the corrugated outline and pedestal slot with a soft pencil onto the laundry paper.

3. Lay the board along one of the borders of your traced design outline on the laundry paper and, using the plywood board as a ruler, draw in a line along the other edge of the plywood strip. Using this new line as a guide along which to place the edge of the 5-inch plywood strip, draw the next line, and so on. When you have drawn the lines in one direction (horizontal or vertical), use a straight side of the design perpendicular to the lines you have just drawn to draw cross lines in like manner. Olé! You have your 5-inch squared grid.

4. The next step is to plot points on the big grid using the small grid as a guide. The best way to avoid distortion is to hang the large grid on a wall. Before you hang it, tape strips of waxed paper to the top of the wall, close to the ceiling, with masking tape, letting the wax paper fall vertically and overlap slightly. Then cut the strips a bit above the floor and join them into one large piece with Scotch tape. This will protect the wall and its paint job.

5. Now place a series of short pieces of masking tape, 3 to 4 inches long, at the top vertically from the masking tape holding the wax-paper strips onto the wall. Run a piece of masking tape all the way across these vertical strips horizontally, which will hold the wax paper to the wall. Do not tape the bottom or the sides of the wax paper yet. Be sure that all of the wall that will be under your design is covered by wax paper.

6. For the next step you will need a friend. Pre-cut some masking-tape strips, 3 to 4 inches in length, and stick them lightly on the wall on each side of the wax paper so they will be handy to pick up. Standing on a chair or a ladder positioned in the center of the wax paper and with your arms outstretched, hold up your large laundry-paper grid. Have your companion eyeball the grid to see that the coordinates are horizontal and vertical. Ask your helper to get up on another chair at one end of the design paper and stick a piece of the masking tape to the laundry paper and to the wall — not to the waxed paper! Then have him move to the other side of the design grid and tape the other side to the wall. There should be no sagging at the top of the design paper.

7. When the design is smooth, put a masking-tape strip all across the top of the design paper attached to the wall. Put short pieces vertically across the horizontal tape and attach these to the wall above the paper but not on top of the vertical tapes holding up the wax paper. Run another piece of tape horizontally across the upper portions of the last-positioned vertical tapes. This will really attach these two papers to the wall independently of each other.

8. Lightly tape the wax paper to the wall at the sides and bottom. Then do the same for the design paper. Small ½-inch spot tapes will do this. Don't tape it all across the bottom or up and down, because from time to time you will have to smooth out the ripples that result from working on the paper. If the tape has to be pulled off, don't strip it off straight back over the wax or design paper: this will pick the papers up and tear them. Start the tape and pull it close to the wall at right angles. The horizontal tape at the top should be pulled vertically upward (or, in any case, away from the center of the paper), and the vertical strips should be pulled at right angles to the right or left. Slowly!

9. When the papers are flat and smooth, you are ready to plot the points on the large grid. Use a light pencil at first until you get the swing of it. To get smooth lines, don't use your fingers to move the pencil: hold it rigidly and use wrist motions. Go over your pencil lines with a felt-tipped pen. If your design is for a rug, use plenty of pressure on the felt-pen ink, because transferring the design onto a rug-backing cloth requires flipping the design over and retracing it on the reverse side onto the cloth.

TRACING LARGE DESIGNS ON THE CLOTH

1. Buy a mattress board to serve as a base. (The single-bed size will do for maps and smaller projects.)

2. Purchase cloth of sufficient width and length to fit your full-scale design plus an additional 25 percent for each vertical and horizontal dimension. If the cloth isn't wide enough, join two strips with a sewing machine (see above).

3. If your home has wall-to-wall carpeting or a single carpet large enough to cover your full-scale drawing, pin the background cloth onto the carpet on three sides to keep it from slipping (Figure 8-14). Stretch it until it lies flat and taut on the carpet. On the fourth side, pin down the background cloth, but leave enough space between the pins so that you can slip the mattress board underneath it. If you don't have a carpet of sufficient size, tape eight layers of flattened newspaper covered with wax paper to a hard-surfaced floor as a substitute. This also adds sponginess, which is needed under the cloth to help keep the carbon from slipping and bunching in front of the wheel. Use masking tape to hold the various materials to the floor. Floors are now made of vinyl instead of wood, and you just don't stick thumb tacks into that armor plate!

8-14.

4. Attach a strip of 2-inch masking tape around the perimeter of the cloth on four sides about an inch from the edges (Figure 8-15). Tack one corner of the cloth with masking tape and place a heavy object on that corner. Then, exerting enough pull on the cloth away from the secured corner to remove wrinkles, strip the taut side of the cloth with 2-inch masking tape. Proceed in this fashion on the other three sides. Do not put any masking tape in the area on the cloth where tracing is to be done. Again, the fourth side should be open to slip in the mattress board.

8-15.

5. Lay the large pieces of carbon paper on top of the background cloth and tape them together very lightly (so carbon doesn't get on the cloth) with No. 810 Scotch Tape to make one big piece to cover the tracing area (Figure 8-16). Make sure that you have the coated surface of the carbon paper next to the cloth.

6. At this point the background cloth should be secured so it won't slip. On top of the cloth you have the carbon and the pattern. Slip the mattress board under the background material if you are not using newspapers on a wood floor (Figure 8-17). If the pattern has long sweeping lines (like the Bird Rug), use a pattern wheel to cut through the design on the laundry paper. Always place your hand behind the pattern wheel as you progress with the motion of the wheel on the design and press down to keep the design from slipping in the direction the wheel is going, which would cause it to bunch up (Figure 8-18). Don't use a pattern wheel on intricate details; use a very hard lead pencil instead. If the cloth next to the carbon paper is going to be viewed in the finished work, be careful not to smudge it. Dirty hands will also really louse up your project. To avoid dirtying cloth and thread, cut an elliptical hole in some smooth, non-abrasive-weave cloth and use it as a surgeon's keyhole (Figure 8-19). Slip the mattress board around under the cloth until all of the design has been transferred.

8-17.

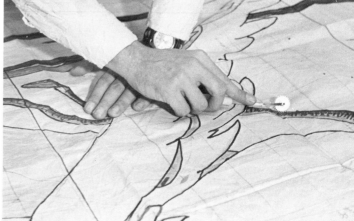
8-18.

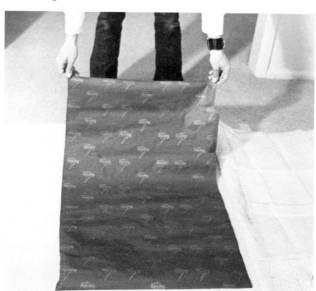
8-16.

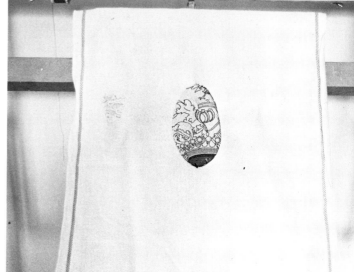
8-19.

POTTY PEDESTAL PERIMETER POSITIONING

With a highboy or lowboy tank at its back, depending on the vintage of the facility, a potty pedestal is usually positioned from 6 to 9 inches from the wall, facing forward as a whole in accordance with all good practices of equitation.

Allowing for the potty pedestal in your cloth is really very simple. All you are doing is sewing onto the background material a piece of muslin cloth that extends from 2 inches inside the perimeter of the pedestal to 2 inches outside the design area of the rug. This is how it is done:

1. Before the background cloth is put on the frame, machine stitch 5/8 inch *inside* the traced perimeter of the pedestal design with a black thread to prevent raveling (Figure 8-20).

2. Cut a rectangular piece of heavy, unbleached muslin 6½ inches wide and long enough to extend the above distances (4 inches) plus the distance your pedestal stands out from the wall. For instance, if the back of the pedestal stands 9 inches from the wall, add 2 inches inside the pedestal contour plus 2 inches outside the rug design, and your piece of muslin should be 13 inches by 6½ inches.

3. Machine stitch in visible black thread around the four sides of the muslin rectangle ¼ inch in from its edge to prevent raveling.

4. Along each 13-inch side of the muslin piece and in 1 inch from the border of the cloth, draw two lines (E-F and G-H in Figure 8-20) with a sharp-pointed, fine-tipped, *red* felt pen. These two lines should be 4¼ inches apart.

5. Meanwhile, at the potty-pedestal design, on the side you will be walking on draw line J-K in red on the background cloth 2 inches in from the back line of the potty pedestal to connect the black, stitched-in, antiraveling lines and continue onto the edges of the pedestal contour. This line will be your guideline, upon which all the following steps are based, so it should be parallel with the edge of the rug design. It will also be the guideline upon which to line up the edge of the muslin (line B-D in Figure 8-20).

6. Somewhere towards the center of the back of the pedestal (line J-K), determine where a line would pass through a simple part of the rug design (two sections that would appear to be joined when simply abutted to each other). Draw a black-pencil line perpendicular to line J-K toward the edge of the design (which is the same as the wall line of the rug), and extend it all the way to the border of the background material. This line is labeled R-S in Figure 8-20.

7. Draw red lines extending from J-K to the border of the background material ¼ inch on either side of the line R-S and parallel to it. These two lines are M-N and O-P in the Figure 8-20. You now have two sets of red lines that will end up perpendicular to the wall line (E-F and G-H, 4½ inches apart, on the muslin piece; M-N and O-P, ½ inch apart, on the background cloth).

8. The next big deal is to pin the muslin onto the background cloth so lines E-F and B-D on the muslin will lie directly on top of lines M-N and J-K, respectively, on the background cloth; and G-H, on top of O-P. Using J-K as a border for the end of the muslin piece (line B-D), machine sew E-F on top of M-N with red thread; and G-H on top of O-P. Doublestitch or backstitch at E, F, G, and H. Make sure that the warp and weft threads of the muslin are parallel to the warp and weft threads of the background cloth.

9. Stitch the muslin to the background cloth from J-K to the edge of the cloth and ¾ inch outside the red lines E-F and G-H. Stitch close to the edges of the muslin (lines A-B and C-D), preferably in black so as not to confuse these lines with the red ones. The muslin from the two red lines to the black lines must lie flat on the background cloth, as punches will come through both layers (muslin and monk's cloth) in working the design from the other side of the cloth. Any slackness of the muslin will impair the uniformity of the work.

10. What you should have now is a tunnel of muslin (Figure 8-20, upper right). Place this tunnel downward so you cannot see it when the background cloth is attached to the frame, allowing it to hang loose under the working area. Don't cross the two red machine-sewn lines, which are M-N and O-P on the other side of the background cloth. Punch exactly along these red lines, occasionally checking to ensure that you have not punched through the cloth of the tunnel and that the tunnel still hangs free.

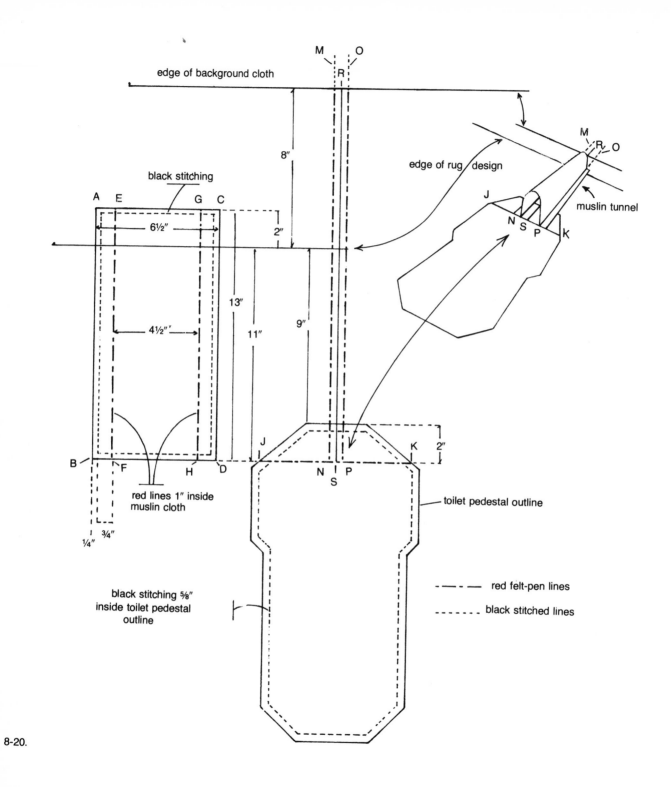

edge of background cloth

black stitching

A E G C

6½"

8"

2"

13"

4½"

11"

9"

M O

R

edge of rug design

M R O

muslin tunnel

J

N S P K

B F H D

red lines 1" inside
muslin cloth

¾"

¼"

J K 2"

N P
S

toilet pedestal outline

black stitching ⅝"
inside toilet pedestal
outline

red felt-pen lines

black stitched lines

8-20.

ATTACHING CLOTH TO AN ADJUSTABLE FRAME

Instead of sporting bruised knuckles from stretching a piece of cloth by hand, you can use one of man's most felicitous inventions, the screw (Figures 8-1 and 8-2). Here is how to do it:

    1. Using a small stapler (Swingline No. 101), attach the background cloth with six or eight small staples to the 1¼-inch dowel on the far side of the frame from which you will be working so that the design is visible to you. (This dowel arrangement is shown in Figure 8-21). These small-staple attachments get the cloth in a position where you can deal with it; without them, it will keep slipping through the frame. The staples are withdrawn almost immediately, so they should not be shot in flush to the frame. Tilt the face of the stapler, where the staples come out, slightly up on one side. This will allow the staple to go into the dowel loosely so that the needle-nose pliers can be slipped under for fast pulling (Figure 8-23).

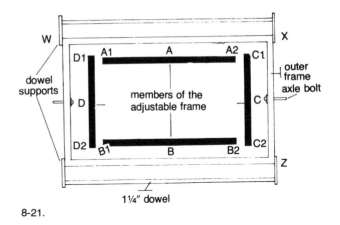

8-21.

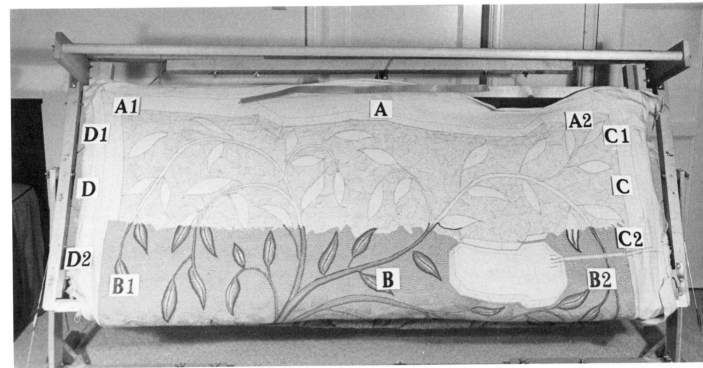

8-22.

119

2. The design will remain inside the four adjustable bars of the inner frame A1-A2, B1-B2, C1-C2, and D1-D2 (Figure 8-22). (To get the right tension, pull these bars toward the rigid outer frame (WXYZ) by tightening the bolts.) Next, align a thread line along the 1¼-inch dowel. When the cloth is rolled up on this dowel, tighten the wing nuts at the ends of the dowel so that the cloth won't spin off and a little pull is needed to unwind it.

3. Pull the cloth across both the rigid and the adjustable frames, using the same method to position it straight on the dowel, that is, using one thread line for the whole length of the lower dowel. Attach the cloth by shooting small staples about 1 inch apart all across the lower dowel.

4. Roll the dowel nearest to you as you sit at the frame until the bottom of the design, which includes the design background, is 1½ to 2 inches above the adjustable bar B1-B2.

5. Turn the whole revolving element of the frame over so that the underside of the cloth shows. Make the inner, adjustable-frame bar B1-B2 parallel to the rigid-frame side Y-Z by loosening or tightening the bolts on the threaded rods, which are shown in Figure 8-24. B1-B2 should be at least 4 inches from Y-Z all along its length, and it should be maintained at that distance by loosening or tightening the bolts so that when you pull the B1-B2 bar towards the center of the frame, the distance between B1-B2 and Y-Z is constant at 4 inches all along its length.

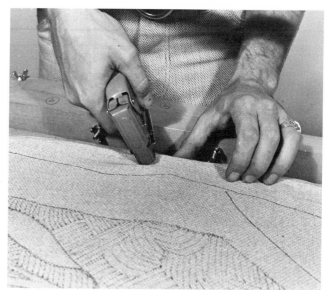

8-23.

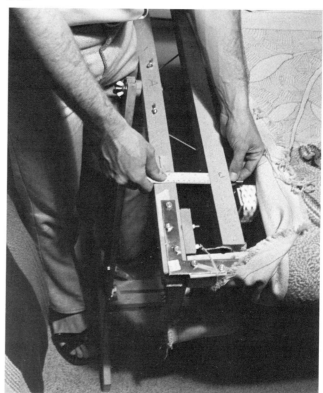

8-24.

120

6. Go around the frame and position A1-A2 in like manner in relation to W-X, that is, 4 inches apart.

7. At the sides of the frame, position the bolts so that D1-D2 is parallel to W-Y and C1-C2 is parallel to X-Z as close to the center of the frame as possible (Figure 8-25).

8. Make sure that D1-D2 and C1-C2 do not extend into the area of your design. Shoot three or four staples through the three-ply gummed paper and the background cloth midway between D1 and D2 at D (Figure 8-26).

9. Move around the frame and pick up the cloth midway between C1 and C2 at C. While exerting a fair amount of pull, shoot three staples at C, as above. Make sure that your design will not extend over bar C1-C2; if it does, you will have to tighten up the bolts on bar D1-D2 and C1-C2 to make the design equidistant from the rigid-frame elements W-Y and X-Z and inside the inner faces of D1-D2 and C1-C2.

10. Move to the corner at D1. Grab the cloth and, maintaining the same thread line that has been established at D, pull the cloth by hand toward D1. Through the cloth and the three-ply gummed paper, shoot three staples at D1.

11. Move to D2. Maintaining the same thread line established above (now at D and D1), shoot three staples through gummed paper along D1-D2 at D2.

12. Perform the same operations listed in steps 10 and 11 at both ends of the bar C1-C2.

13. Because you have set the cloth at both D2 and C2, there should be a thread line that coincides with the outer edges of B1-B2. To check this, trace a thread from a point at D2 across the frame to C2; the traced thread should fall at the same position at the end of C1-C2 as at D1-D2. Follow this thread line across the cloth and staple the cloth at B (in the middle of the B1-B2 bar) through the gummed paper. This is a permanent attachment.

14. Perform the same stapling maneuver at the other side of the frame to attach the cloth at A. These two attachments will keep the cloth from bowing in when you do the next step.

8-26.

8-25.

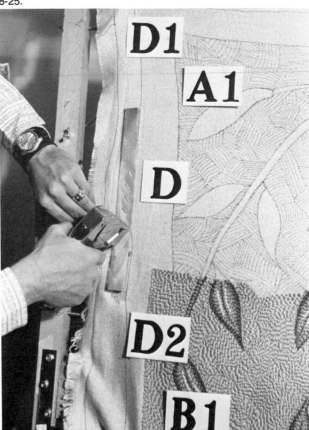

15. Using the ratcheted box wrench *always* on the inner side of the adjustable frame, tighten the bolts on the C1-C2 bar and on the D1-D2 bar. Keep both bars parallel to and at equal distances from the side of the rigid frame nearest to them, tightening all four bolts alternately (like lugs on a car wheel) until the cloth is taut.

16. You have now obtained lateral tension. Next, staple through gummed paper at A1 and A2, maintaining the same thread line established at A. Staple through gummed paper with heavy-duty staples all along A1-A2. These staples will be permanent throughout your work on this section of the design (Figure 8-27).

17. Do the same along B1-B2.

18. Stop for a cold beer. It is time to brag about what you have done. You have the cloth stapled all the way across A1-A2 and B1-B2. The cloth is also attached at D1 and D2 and at C1 and C2. All you need to do now is to remove and restaple the cloth at D and C along the same thread lines that have been established at D1, D2, C1, and C2 with heavy, permanent staples through three-ply paper. To make this easier, release some of the tension on the nuts along one of the vertical bars.

19. Start tightening bars A1-A2 and B1-B2. When the cloth starts to strain at points D1, D2, C1, and C2, take out the staples at those points.

20. Continue to tighten the A1-A2 and the B1-B2 bars. When the tension in the very center of the design becomes quite taut, staple the cloth through the gummed tape with heavy-duty staples, starting at midpoint D and toward the ends D1 and D2 and maintaining the thread line established at the center point D. Use either your hands or canvas pliers to pull the cloth onto the thread line (Figure 8-28).

21. Do the same along C1-C2. This is the hardest part of the whole maneuver. If you have difficulty pulling the thread line up to C1-C2, release the bolts a little along C1-C2.

Olé! You are now through attaching. Tension can be varied now simply by loosening or tightening the bolts.

8-27.

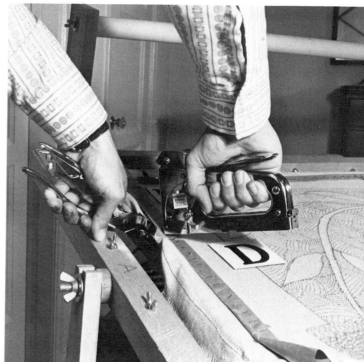

8-28.

BALANCING THE CLOTH

If you are going to make a large punch rug or any other weighty project that can be rolled onto the dowel rollers, creating an off-balance situation as the work progresses and becomes heavier, you are well advised to have sired a son. Each boy, somewhere in some closet along with his high-school-band uniform, BB gun, rock collection, moribund sneakers, chemistry set, embalmed frogs, electric guitar, rope ladder, and reverb amplifier has a brand-new, dust-covered set of muscle-building weights. From time to time, lay these weights on the outer edge of the wooden frame away from the weighty rolled-up stitchery, increasing them with the increasing weight of the roll until you balance it. When you have the proper balance, bolt these weights onto the wooden frame as shown in Figures 8-29 and 8-30. This way the unbalanced frame won't get away from you and slap you across the room.

8-29.

8-30.

PUNCHING LARGE PROJECTS

Be a two-fisted puncher. When you start out punching, whether you are right- or left-handed, your best hand knows absolutely nothing about the punching motion. From the outset, use both of your hands equally for punching. There are directions on your design, the left-to-right directions, for which your left hand (if you are right-handed) is infinitely more suited than your right. Learn to switch hands in using your needle. They will both learn at the same time with equal efficiency, and it will save hours of getting up and walking around to the head of the frame to continue to use your strong hand in the opposite direction or cutting the yarn and starting over another line in the same direction. It will also cut down on chapped lips as your tongue will stay inside more.

In the old silent movies the real "risky" scene that used to knock them down in the aisles showed an unsuspecting, dumb comedian pick up a piece of string lying on the ground and innocently walk off, not knowing that the yarn was the end of a knit skirt, inside of which stood some hotcha chick. It is hard to imagine the havoc that occurred when the skirt unraveled all the way to her knee. Wowee! If you leave a strand of yarn hanging off the edge of your work and it unravels, wowee will be mild. The way to avoid this problem is to start the border of your project about 2 inches *inside* the design; then punch out to the border before continuing around (Figure 8-31).

To keep stitches uniform, tension must be uniform. If soft spots appear in the cloth during the progress of the work, they are probably caused by the cloth splitting around a staple. Withdraw the staple involved in the split and restaple the cloth in through the three-ply paper slightly to one side of the tear, using the canvas pliers to pull the cloth back onto the thread line. The adjustable frame overcomes the tedium of restretching cloth.

Large projects such as rugs and wall hangings, which require moving the cloth design on the frame to complete them, end up with a lot of the completed work exposed. After the first section is completed, it should be pulled up on a dowel. In working the subsequent areas, the frame will have to be flipped over constantly, which can cause the completed work to rub against your knees continually. This rubbing can pull stitches out of the design, but worse, it will surely fuzz the stitched areas with rubbed-off lint, which requires hours and hours of pruning to remove. This dilemma can be almost completely overcome by stapling heavy plastic bags or cotton sheets over the finished part of the work (Figure 8-32). I use plastic because it is slick and will slip on contact with outside materials, whereas another cloth, such as pants material, would sheer the finished work whenever you change the position of your legs. I roll the plastic around the rolled-up, finished work and attach it with staples to the nearest wood members of the frames. If you cannot get wide pieces of heavy plastic, use large yardwork-refuse bags.

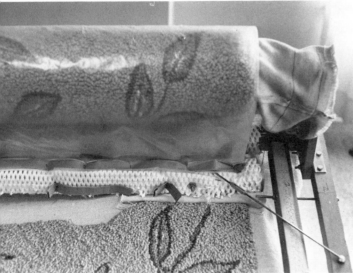

8-31.

SECURING THE STITCHES IN A RUG

In rug making, it is necessary to cement the stitches with a back coating so that they will not work themselves out from the patter of little feet or the snags from big heels. A product that I have used to good effect for cementing is Robert's Carpet-seaming Adhesive, Latex-Base Type No. 41–0502. To apply it, place wax paper under the edges to guard the floor from the latex goo and use a piece of old carpeting for smearing it on (Figure 8-33). Pour out only a little at a time, as it turns to rubber rapidly. To enjoy this rug after all your labors, open the window when you spread the goo on the back of it. The solvent is carbon tetrachloride, which will play hob with the most prohibitionistic of livers.

The proper sequence of finishing a rug is to (1) Scotchguard it, (2) apply the rubber-cement backing, and (3) tape it. If you do (2) or (3) first, the Scotchguarding will melt the stickum of the cement and the tape, and you've had it! It will take days for the stickum on the back to dry and for the tape to restick.

8-32.

8-33.

OPENING THE PEDESTAL AREA

If you get to this page and are still outside of the Laughing Academy, you are not only a trained carpenter, artist, archaeologist, genealogist, historian, philologist, and philosopher, but an accomplished third- or fourth-echelon cusser. It is now time to take your masterpiece off the frame and just sit there and luxuriate in an aura of well-deserved conceit. If, perchance, the rug you are preening yourself over is a bathroom rug, there are a few minor damnabilities to perform.

1. With the loops of the rug up, cut the muslin tunnel lengthwise. Separate the two pieces and expose the background cloth (Figure 8-34).

2. Cut the background cloth along the pencil line, which is line R-S in Figure 8-21 (Figure 8-35). Extend the cut 4 inches inside the pedestal area to allow cutting room.

3. Starting at the end of the 2-inch cut inside the pedestal area, cut the unworked cloth around the pedestal slot, then trim this cloth hole to within 1½ inches of the rug on all sides (Figure 8-36).

8-34.

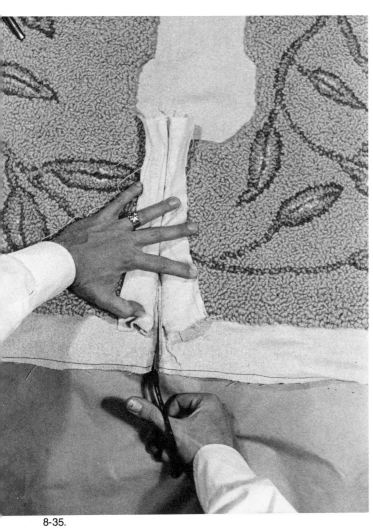

8-35.

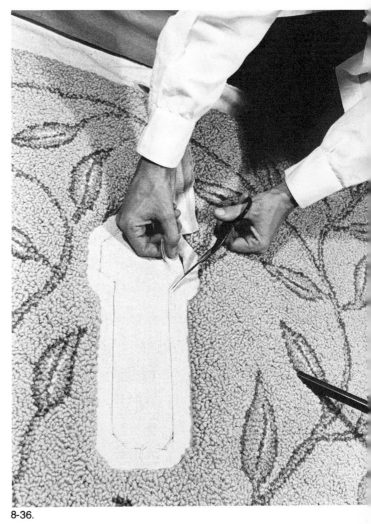

8-36.

4. Now turn the rug over, loops down. Cut to within ¼ inch of the rug line, bisecting the angles in the pedestal slot at all angles (Figure 8-37).

5. Cut around the perimeter of the rug to within 1½ inches of the loops (Figure 8-38). Bisect the angles in the cloth for the tub and doors (Figure 8-39).

6. Flip over the 1½-inch flaps inside the pedestal area and around the perimeter, exposing the rug edges (Figure 8-40).

8-37.

8-38.

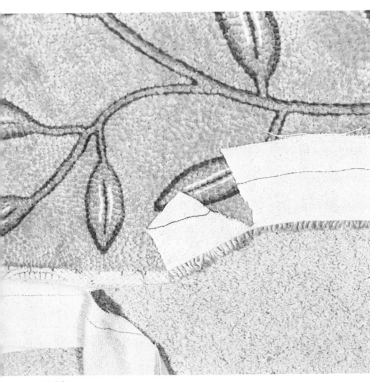

8-39.

8-40.

7. Before taping, square off the loops (Figure 8-41) which tends to overcome curling edges, especially on the perimeter.

8. Tape the perimeter flap up to the cut of the pedestal slot with 2-inch Arno tape before squaring off the muslin flaps (Figure 8-42) and taping them (Figure 8-43).

9. Tape the entire inside of the pedestal perimeter, flap by flap, until it is completed. (To get tension for laying a length of Arno tape on the perimeter, do not stretch it before it is applied: if it is stretched, it will draw up and ripple the perimeter of the rug.)

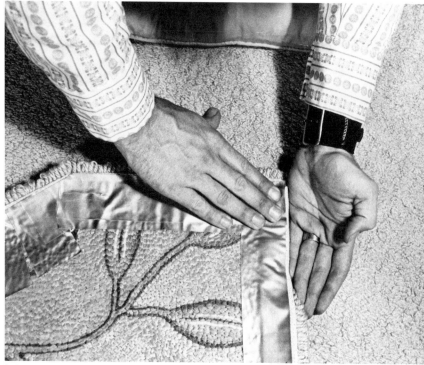

8-41.

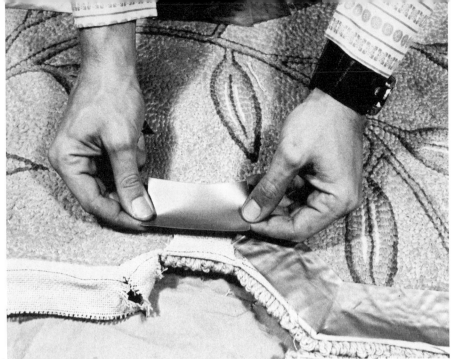

8-42.

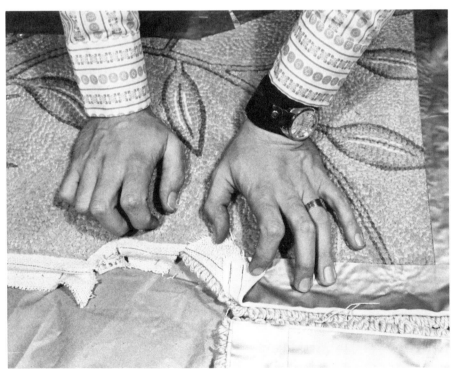

8-43.

To those of us who are trapped in the tentacles of tobacco and bound by the bonds of booze, Peace! Although I can't free you from what the brimstone breathers call the fetters of our flaws nor deliver you from the demonism of your diversions, I can supplant your miscreant suasions with the do-gooders' whack on the tambourine of temperance — the panacea of punchery! But are smoking and swigging really valid vices? When I was young, dancing was even wicked. As was something shouted down to my eight-year-old ears from the pulpit each Sunday called the concupiscence of the flesh, whatever the hell that was supposed to mean. Something that I was told, in no uncertain terms, would lead me through the storms of Hell to the pits of perdition, I now find leads but to the drugstore. Another prime degrader was gambling, excoriated in blue epithets from the altar while in the next breath the lucky winner of the church lottery was congratulated. We all gamble to some extent — that the customs official won't notice the diamonds sparkling in our cavities, that the postparty driver can weather the martini miasma, that The Pill works. Then there are the nebulous sins of coveting. Yet, we honor peacemakers with the coveted Nobel Prize, first-draft seekers with the coveted Heisman Trophy, and writers of better wit than I with the coveted Pulitzer Prize. Coveting is not so much a sin of desire as a desire to aspire. Then there are the committing sins, which are a matter of activating the covet — like pinching (not punching) the company's funds or making out with your neighbor's wife (falling prey to the age-old fantasy that the plural of "spouse" is "spice"). I return to my premise that stitchery can keep you happily free from trouble. I ask you, my friend, if your busy little hands are full of needles and threads, how can they be full of cigarettes, booze, the company's funds . . . or your neighbor's wife?

Index

TT
840
I42

Illes, Robert E.   50048

Men in stitches

DATE			
JAN 22 '81			

© THE BAKER & TAYLOR CO.